NAOKI URASAWA'S

MONSTER

volume 3

Naoki Urasawa's
Monster
Volume 3

VIZ Signature Edition

STORY AND ART BY NAOKI URASAWA

English Adaptation/Agnes Yoshida
Translation/Masaru Noma
Touch-up Art & Lettering/Steve Dutro
Design/Courtney Utt
Editor/Andy Nakatani

Managing Editor/Annette Roman
Director of Production/Noboru Watanabe
Vice President of Publishing/Alvin Lu
Sr. Director of Acquisitions/Rika Inouye
Vice President of Sales & Marketing/Liza Coppola
Publisher/Hyoe Narita

Printed in the U.S.A.

Published by VIZ Media, LLC
P.O. Box 77010
San Francisco, CA 94107

VIZ Signature Edition
10 9 8 7 6 5 4 3 2 1
First printing, June 2006

www.viz.com
store.viz.com

RATED T+ FOR OLDER TEEN

PARENTAL ADVISORY
NAOKI URASAWA'S MONSTER is rated T+ for Older Teen and is recommended for ages 16 and up. This volume contains realistic and graphic violence.

Naoki Urasawa's
Monster
Volume 3
511 Kinderheim

Story and Art by Naoki Urasawa

Jägerhaus
HERE'S YOUR MANHATTAN.
HEY, WHERE'S THE CHERRY?!
HUH?
IT'S NOT A MANHATTAN WITHOUT THE CHERRY!!
OH, SORRY...
YOU BETTER WATCH IT, BUDDY.
SLURP
HUH?
BUSINESS ALWAYS GOES WELL WHEN I'M SUCKING ON ONE OF THESE.

Chapter 1
A Past Erased

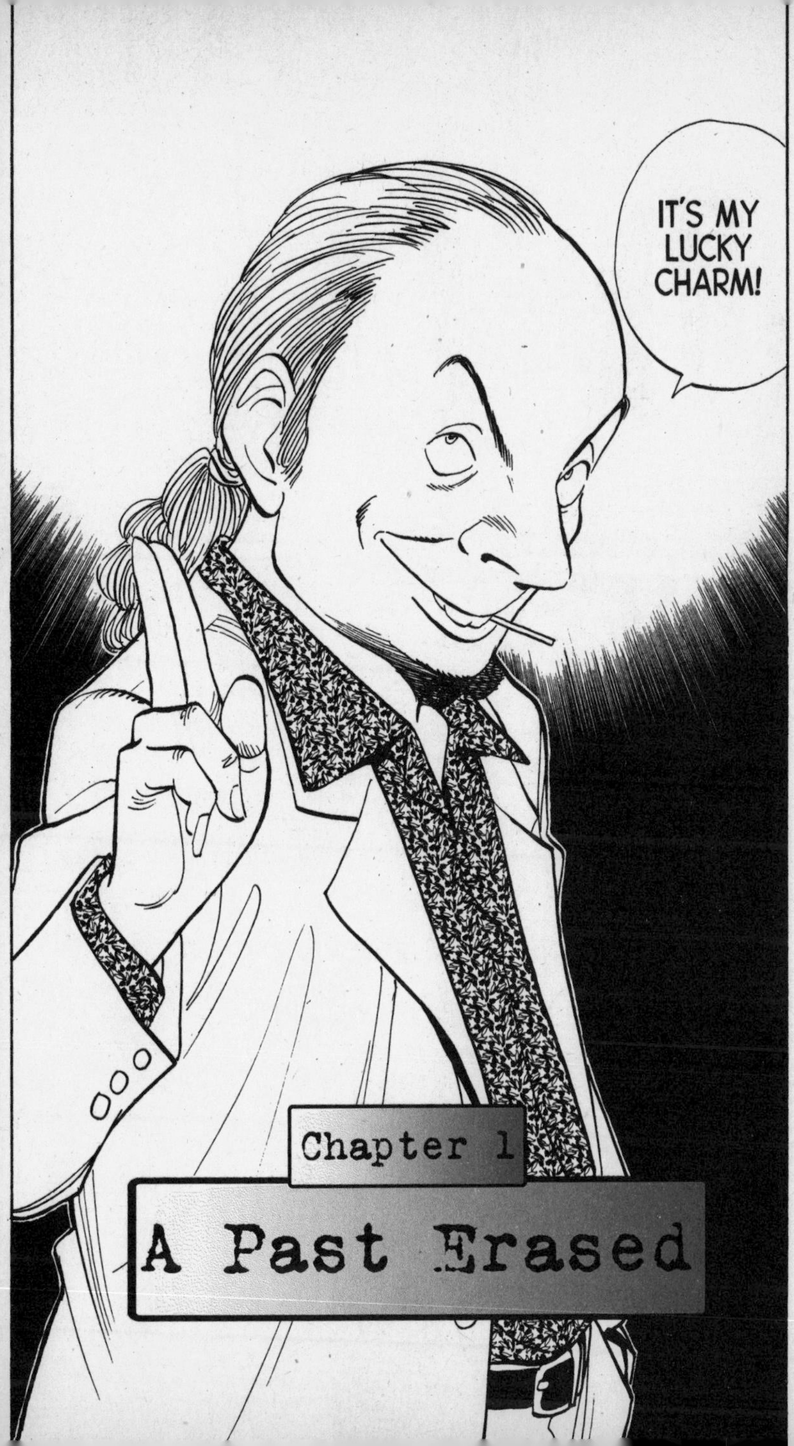
IT'S MY LUCKY CHARM!
Chapter 1
A Past Erased

Verden, Germany
I'VE BEEN CASING CITY COUNCILMAN SPRINGER'S ESTATE FOR QUITE SOME TIME.
I HOPE THERE'S STILL SOME LOOT WORTH TAKING.
KRK
FWP
UMPH ...

GOOD DEAL, GOOD DEAL!
I KNEW IT. THERE'S SOME GOOD FURNITURE LEFT.
IT'S A FIVE-FINGER FREE-FOR-ALL!
BUT IS THERE ANYTHING GOOD ENOUGH FOR THE DISCRIMINATING EYE OF OTTO HECKEL?
!!
HMPH! NEVER KNOW WHAT'S GONNA HAPPEN.
SPRINGER WAS THE SHOE-IN CANDIDATE FOR STATE GOVERNOR, BUT YOU CAN'T TAKE OFFICE IF YOU AND YOUR WIFE ARE SHOT DEAD.
I DON'T *EVER* WANT TO BE OUTLINED IN CHALK.
ANYWAYS... GOTTA GET THIS JOB DONE BEFORE THE CHERRY IN MY MOUTH DISINTEGRATES.
SHUF
SHUF

THE SAFE SHOULD BE IN HERE...
WHY AM I GETTING THE CHILLS?!
I DON'T LIKE THIS FEELING.
IS SOME-ONE IN THERE...?
HAH! HOW COULD THAT BE?
ISN'T LIKE ME TO BE CHICKEN.
KCHK
!!

DONT MOVE!! HANDS BEHIND YOUR HEAD!!
SO YOU'RE BEHIND ME...
DAMN BARTENDER. WHY'D HE HAVE TO FORGET THE CHERRY?
IT'S ALL SQUASHED UP NOW, TOO.
THIS HOUSE IS BAD LUCK.
PUT YOUR HANDS UP!!
OKAY, OKAY.
LET ME SLIDE ON THIS ONE, OFFICER.
I HAVEN'T TAKEN ANYTHING YET.
I'M NOT A COP.
WHAT ?
YOU'RE A THIEF, TOO?!
THEN PUT THAT THING DOWN. I'M UNARMED.
BESIDES, YOU MAY NOT BELIEVE ME, BUT IT'S HARD TO HIT SOMEONE WHEN YOU'RE TOO CLOSE.

I WON'T MISS.
WHO IS THIS GUY...?
HE'S WORSE THAN THE COPS.
PEE PO PEE PO
!!
IT'S THE COPS!! YOU SCREWED THIS JOB UP!!
!!
PEE PO PEE PO
DON'T HAVE TIME TO CHAT!! I'M OUTTA HERE!!

DON'T FOLLOW ME!! YOU'LL GET IN THE WAY!!
DAMN!
HEY!!
STOP FOLLOWING ME!! GO THE OTHER WAY!!
I SAID, DON'T FOLLOW ME!!
TODAY JUST AIN'T MY DAY!!

HE ESCAPED!! SECURE THE AREA!!
IT'S THE MAN IN THE PAPER. HE CAME ASKING ABOUT THE INCIDENT THAT OCCURRED ON THIS ESTATE.
IT'S HIM FOR SURE!!
PANT
PANT
PANT
PANT
AH-HAH! I THOUGHT I RECOGNIZED YOU. YOU'RE IN ALL THE PAPERS...
HUF
HUF
YOU'RE WANTED FOR QUESTIONING IN CONNECTION WITH COUNCILMAN SPRINGER'S MURDER!!
PANT
PANT

YOU'RE A FOOL FOR GOING TO THAT PLACE.
YOU'RE A THIEF?
THAT'S RIGHT!
I'M NOT A KILLER LIKE YOU. I GOT A GOOD HEAD ON MY SHOULDERS.
I'M LOOKING FOR THE REAL KILLER.
DO YOU KNOW ANYTHING ABOUT WHAT HAPPENED IN THAT HOUSE?
NO, SO GET OUT OF MY FACE. I DON'T WANT ANY TROUBLE.
SEE YA.
...
HEY, DOC!! YOU'RE A TOP SURGEON, RIGHT?
I'VE GOT A GREAT IDEA!

DON'T GET ME WRONG, DOC. I'VE GOT NO INTENTION OF STAYING IN THIS LINE OF BUSINESS.
BEING A THIEF JUST DOESN'T UTILIZE MY FULL POTENTIAL...
IN LIFE, YOU HAVE TO REACH FOR THE GOLDEN RING!!
DO YOU BELIEVE IN FATE, DOC?
.....
I THINK PEOPLE MEET FOR A REASON...
HUH?
WE WERE DESTINED TO TEAM UP.
WHAT?
A LOT OF PEOPLE IN THE UNDERGROUND COMMUNITY NEED SOMEONE LIKE YOU...
PEOPLE WHO CAN'T GO TO REGULAR DOCTORS FOR HELP.

WHAT ARE YOU SAYING?
I'LL BE YOUR MANAGER!
I'LL MAKE YOU THE WORLD'S BEST UNDERGROUND DOCTOR.
I'M TELLING YOU, DOC, THE PAY IS OUT OF THIS WORLD!!
YOU'LL BE A MILLIONAIRE!
H-HEY!
WHERE YOU GOING?!
THERE'S SOMETHING I MUST DO.
WAIT. YOU WANT TO KNOW ABOUT THE MURDERS, RIGHT?
HEH HEH HEH.
I SAW THE KILLER.

WHAT ?!
ARE YOU TELLING THE TRUTH ?!
YOU WANT TO KNOW?
WAS HE A BLOND BOY ABOUT TWENTY YEARS OLD?
WHAT?
TELL ME ABOUT THE KILLER!!
TEAM UP WITH ME AND I'LL TELL YOU ALL ABOUT HIM.
HE'S ON THE THIRD FLOOR.
HOW DO YOU KNOW THIS?
I GOT SMARTS.
I DO MY GROUND-WORK BEFORE I DO ANY JOB.

I CHECKED OUT THE COUNCILMAN'S HOUSE FOR AN ENTIRE MONTH.
THE KILLER CAME RIGHT WHEN I WAS ABOUT TO GO FOR IT.
HE WAS IN AND OUT WITHIN FIFTEEN MINUTES...
I LOOKED THROUGH THE WINDOW AND SAW THAT THE COUNCILMAN AND HIS WIFE WERE DEAD.
I FIGURED I MIGHT BE ABLE TO BLACKMAIL THE MURDERER, SO I FOLLOWED HIM.
WHO IS HE?
NO ONE WORTH SHAKING DOWN, SO I LEFT HIM ALONE.
WHAT?
THAT'S ALL YOU NEED, RIGHT? NOW YOU CAN PROVE YOUR INNOCENCE.
CALL THE POLICE AND TELL THEM.
THEN WE CAN TALK ABOUT OUR FUTURE TOGETHER. OVER A DRINK--
H- HEY!!
CREAK

STOP!! WHAT ARE YOU DOING?! HE'S A MURDERER!! HE'LL KILL YOU!!
SHUF
SHUF
WHAT'S HE THINKING?!
I'M OUT OF HERE!!
SHUF
SHUF
WHAT A WASTE...
AN OPPORTUNITY LIKE THAT IS RARE.
DAMN! I DON'T LIKE TAKING RISKS, BUT...
KNOCK KNOCK
KLIK
CREAK

HI.
HELLO.
IT'S SO HOT TODAY...
I'M...
I'M LOOKING FOR SOMEONE ...
DAMN!!
KNOCK KNOCK
HEY, DOC, YOU ALIVE IN THERE?
CREAK
DOC...

HEY!! HE'S GOT A GUN!!
I USED TO TAKE WALKS... WITH MY MOTHER...
HUH?
...ON SUMMER DAYS LIKE THIS. THERE WAS THIS ROAD ALONGSIDE A FIELD OF SUN-FLOWERS...
...BUT SHE DIED A LONG TIME AGO.
SOMEBODY ASKED YOU TO USE THAT GUN, RIGHT?
A MAN...
A MAN...? YES...AT A BAR.
HE HAD A BIG SMILE...

A BLOND, ABOUT TWENTY ...?
HUH?
YES...
ERICH HAD SUCH A NICE SMILE.
HE'S GOING BY ERICH NOW...
WE MET A FEW TIMES AND BECAME FRIENDS.
HE INVITED ME OVER TO WHERE HE WAS STAYING-- COUNCILMAN SPRINGER'S ESTATE...
WHAT?!
HE LIVED WITH THE COUNCILMAN?
YES, FOR A YEAR. HE WAS LIKE A SON TO THEM.
...
WHAT? I STAKED THEM OUT FOR A MONTH AND I NEVER SAW HIM THERE.
THEY WERE A LOVELY FAMILY.
THIS IS A PICTURE WE TOOK.

BUT...
I COULDN'T FORGIVE HIM.
?
THERE WERE SUNFLOWERS IN THE YARD...
...BUT HE CLEARED THEM OUT FOR A BIGGER DRIVEWAY.
IT WAS TERRIBLE ...
ERICH THOUGHT SO, TOO.
YOU...
YOU KILLED THEM FOR *THAT?!*
ERICH ALSO TOLD ME THAT SPRINGER HAD A MISTRESS. A COUNCILMAN WITH A MISTRESS...
...
ERICH SAID HE WASN'T GOING TO STAY WITH THEM ANYMORE.

HE SAID HE WASN'T A PART OF THAT FAMILY ANYMORE.
THEN HE ASKED ME TO "ERASE THE FAMILY."
HAVING A MISTRESS IS INEXCUSABLE.
MY MOTHER WAS A KEPT WOMAN...
U-UM, HEY...
WOULD YOU HAPPEN TO KNOW...
...WHERE THE SAFE IS?
IT'S UPSTAIRS IN THE LIBRARY.
OKAY!!
DOC, DON'T STICK AROUND HERE FOR TOO LONG!

SLAM
DID YOU KNOW?
YOU CAN ERASE YOUR PAST.
IF YOU DON'T LIKE IT, YOU CAN ERASE IT ALL AWAY...
LIFE CAN BE RESET.
I DON'T AGREE.
YOU CAN TRY TO FORGET, BUT IT CAN NEVER BE ERASED!
YOU'RE RIGHT...
......
WHY DID I EVER THINK IT COULD BE...?
......
WHY DID I THINK I COULD ERASE MY PAST BY PULLING A TRIGGER...?
WHY DID I LISTEN TO HIM?

OUR TALK IS OVER.
PLEASE LEAVE.
...
OH, YES...
YOU'RE DR. TENMA, RIGHT?
!!
HE LEFT A MESSAGE FOR YOU...
...IN THE COUNCIL-MAN'S LIBRARY.
WHAT?!
HE KNEW YOU WOULD COME.
ERICH SAID, "YOUR FATE HAS ALREADY BEEN DECIDED."
GOODBYE...

THAT WAS A BIT HAIRY.
NOW I JUST GOTTA GET TO THAT SAFE...
!!
DOC !!
DAMN IT! THERE GOES MY CHANCE OF USING YOU TO MAKE SOME DOUGH.
HUH?
DOC, DID *YOU*--?!
SUICIDE, *HUH*?
JEEZ...

FLIP FLIP
EVERYTHING'S OVER AFTER YOU'RE DEAD.
NOTHING BEATS LIVING, *EH,* DOC?
YES...
SOMETIMES WHAT YOU SAY MAKES SENSE.
WHAT DO YOU MEAN, "*SOME-TIMES*"?!
SO YOU'RE AFTER THIS KILLER NAMED ERICH OR JOHAN OR WHATEVER.
WHY DON'T YOU FORGET ABOUT THAT AND TEAM UP WITH ME?
WONDER WHY I GOT THE HEEBIE-JEEBIES WHEN I WAS ABOUT TO ENTER THIS ROOM BEFORE...

ガバッ
WHAT THE--?!
SHAKE SHAKE
WHAT'S WRONG, DOC?
SHAKE SHAKE SHAKE
SHAKE SHAKE SHAKE SHAKE

Mein lieber Dr. Tenma
Sehen Sie mich!
Sehen Sie mich!
Das Monstrum in meinem
Selbst ist
So groß
geworden!
"DR. TENMA, LOOK AT ME! LOOK AT ME! THE MONSTER INSIDE ME IS GETTING BIGGER."

JOHAN...
HE'S ENJOYING THIS...

HEY, DOC!! WAIT UP!!
LISTEN TO ME, DOC!! HEY, I'M TALKING TO YOU!!

Chapter 2

Lawyer's Rules

GOOD NEWS, DOC! OTTO HECKEL DOES IT AGAIN! YOU'RE GONNA THANK ME.
YOU'RE GONNA KEEP YOUR PROMISE, RIGHT? I'VE LINED UP AN OPERATION FOR 15,000 MARKS!
THAT'S 15,000 MARKS!
I NEVER SAID I'D TEAM UP WITH YOU!
HEY!
YOU NEED MONEY TO RUN FROM THE COPS, RIGHT?
!!

GET IN THE CAR!
...
DON'T EVEN THINK ABOUT IT. I ALREADY SWIPED YOUR GUN.
THIS IS OUR CLIENT. HE'LL ESCORT YOU TO THE PATIENT.
I WAS PAID HALF UP FRONT.
YOU GET PAID THE OTHER HALF IF YOU'RE SUCCESSFUL.
GET GOING ALREADY.
ドン

I'LL HOLD ON TO YOUR STUFF. IF YOU WANT IT BACK, DO YOUR JOB, GET THE MONEY, AND COME TO FRANK'S TAVERN ON GRASTEN.
...
NOW, GO EARN YOUR KEEP!
HAH! THIS IS TOO EASY.
NOW THAT I GOT PAID, AND HE'S WORKING...
IT'S TIME TO DRINK!
COUNSELOR! EVERYTHING'S GOING TO BE FINE. I BROUGHT A DOCTOR.

PANT
PANT
PANT
HUF
HUF
I'M COUNTING ON YOU, DOCTOR...
YOU MUST STOP THE BLEEDING.
YOUR AXILLARY ARTERY IS DAMAGED.
YES... YOU MUST HELP ME...
YOU DON'T HAVE ANY EQUIPMENT.
N-NO. WE DIDN'T HAVE TIME...

I COULDN'T DO IT EVEN IF I HAD THE PROPER EQUIPMENT.
HUH ...?
TAKE HIM TO A DOCTOR IN A FULLY EQUIPPED HOSPITAL.
IF WE COULD, WE WOULD. *YOU* MUST HELP HIM!!
WHEN WAS HE SHOT?
NO QUESTIONS !!
HURRY UP AND SAVE HIM!!
...
WAS IT ABOUT FOUR HOURS AGO...?

YOU WERE INVOLVED IN THIS MORNING'S TERRORIST INCIDENT!!
WHAT IF WE WERE?
Y-YEAH!! WHAT'RE YOU GOING TO DO?!
I'M NOT HELPING YOU!
WHA --?
WHAT ?!
I DON'T HELP INDISCRIMINATE KILLERS!

DO YOU REALIZE THE SITUATION YOU'RE IN!?
HELP HIM! DO IT OR DIE!!
...
CALM DOWN ...
DOCTOR, OUR FRIENDS WILL BE HERE SOON.
PLEASE, AT LEAST JUST STOP THE BLEEDING.
SHUF
SHUF
?

WHAT THE HELL?! DO YOU WANT TO DIE?!
I TOLD YOU TO CALM DOWN.
B-BUT, COUNSEL-OR...
MY LIFE IS IN HIS HANDS...
IF I DIE, *THEN* YOU CAN KILL HIM.
Frank's
FREE TONIGHT? HOW ABOUT DINNER?

HAH! YOU'RE UP TO SOMETHING!!
OF COURSE I AM!
I'M THINKING ABOUT WHAT KIND OF DRESSES WOULD BEST SUIT YOU LADIES...
...AND WHAT KIND OF DRESSES WOULD BEST *UNSUIT* YOU!
YOU'RE SO SILLY!
HA HA HA! BARTENDER, ANOTHER ROUND FOR THE LADIES!!
AND ONE FOR YOU, TOO!
HECKEL! SEEMS YOU'RE DOING WELL.
YEAH, BUSINESS IS--
!!

...
MR. GLAUS... I, UH--
WHAT A COINCIDENCE...
WHO KNEW WE'D RUN INTO YOU HERE?
WHERE'S THE MONEY?
UH... Y-YEAH...
WHAT?
WE'RE NOT RUNNING A CHARITY. YOU OWE US!
THAT'S 250,000 MARKS PLUS 50,000 MARKS FOR INTEREST!
WELL, YOU SEE...I WANT TO PAY YOU BACK, BUT--
HEH HEH HEH...
I'M GLAD YOU FEEL THAT WAY.
BREAK HIS ARMS.
AAHHH!

O-OKAY!
I'LL PAY UP!!
THAT'S A GOOD BOY.
GIVE ME ANOTHER MONTH...
BREAK HIS LEGS, TOO!
THIS MORNING, A TERRORIST ATTACK AT ERFURT STATION...
AAHH!!
...LEFT TWELVE DEAD AND TWO SERIOUSLY WOUNDED.
GNN
THE TARGET OF THE ATTACK, FREDRICH WANZ, PRESIDENT OF GWE, DIED IN TRANSIT TO THE HOSPITAL.
OWWWW!!
WITNESSES HAVE HELPED TO IDENTIFY THE SUSPECTS...
WAIT A MINUTE! ARGH!!
!!
...AS MAX STEINDORF AND KARL BLUNT.
GWE IS OFFERING 300,000 MARKS FOR ANY INFORMATION LEADING TO ARRESTS OF THE TERRORISTS.
WHAT A TRAGEDY.
GASP!

I-IT'S THEM!!
HUH?
I-I CAN PAY YOU!!
I KNOW WHERE THEY ARE!!
WHAT?
I'LL TELL YOU WHERE THEY ARE AND WE'LL BE EVEN!!
I'LL BREAK YOUR NECK IF YOU'RE LYING.
TRUST ME! I'M NOT LYING!!
WAIT, TENMA'S OVER THERE...
OH, WELL...
HEY ...
PANT
PANT
YOU CALLED ME AN INDIS-CRIMINATE KILLER.

PANT
PANT
I AM NOT AN INDISCRIMINATE KILLER.
WHAT I DID HAD MEANING...
...
COUNSELOR, DON'T TALK SO MUCH.
HURRY UP AND HELP HIM!!
IT'S OKAY, MR. SECRETARY.
PANT
I-I DON'T MIND DYING NOW.
PANT
WHAT ?!
...
NOW THAT FREDRICH WANZ, THE PRESIDENT OF GWE, IS DEAD...
I-I CAN REST IN PEACE...I FEEL MUCH BETTER...
PANT
PANT
COUNSELOR...

I WAS A LAWYER IN EAST GERMANY. MY FRIEND HERE WAS A POLITICAL SECRETARY.
THE WALL CAME DOWN AND WE LOST OUR JOBS... WE'RE TRUE EXPATRIATES.
DO YOU KNOW WHAT IT'S LIKE FOR US...?
DO YOU, MR. UNDER-GROUND DOCTOR?
SCREW UNIFICATION. SCREW CAPITALISM!
WHAT ABOUT US? HOW WILL WE LIVE?!
AFTER THE WALL FELL, GWE CAME TO THE EAST WITH THEIR BIG FUNDING.
THEY STRONG-ARMED THEIR WAY IN AND BUILT SO MANY FACTORIES ON OUR LAND... STEPPED ON OUR PRIDE...
IN *OUR* COUNTRY...
I DON'T NEED *YOU* TELLING ME WHAT TO DO...
I WAS PROUD TO SHOOT HIM.
...

I WAS PROUD...
...TO SHOOT HIM.
COUN-SELOR...
IT'S COLD ...
WHAT ?
I'M COLD...
H-HANG ON! OUR FRIENDS WILL BE HERE SOON!!
THEY WON'T COME...
WHAT ?

I HAVE A FEELING...
...THEY WON'T BE COMING.
...
HELP THE COUNSELOR !!
DO IT NOW!!
HURRY !!
OR ELSE I'LL KILL YOU!!
I DON'T WANT TO DIE...
HUH ?
I DON'T WANT TO DIE...

I DON'T WANT TO DIE...
HEY!
SHUF
SHUF
ARE YOU AFRAID?

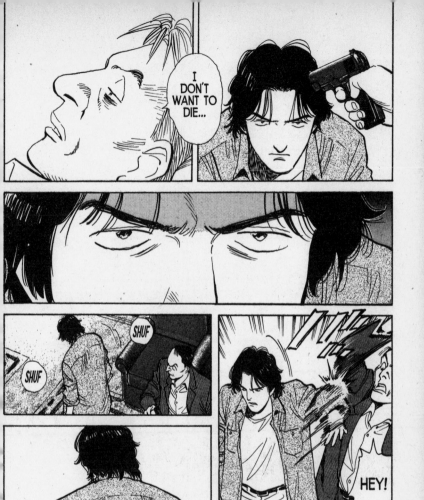

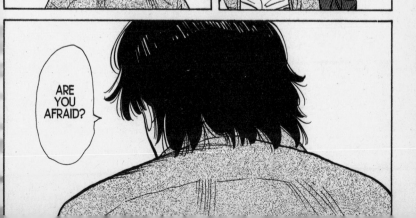

ARE YOU AFRAID OF DYING?!
SHUF
SHUF
PANT
PANT
THAT'S HOW *THEY* DIED...!!
...THE TWELVE PEOPLE YOU KILLED!!
DO YOU UNDERSTAND WHAT IT REALLY MEANS TO KILL SOMEONE?!

DISIN-FECTANT AND SCISSORS!!
WHAT?
THAT'S NOT TOO MUCH TO ASK FOR, IS IT?!
UH, SURE... SO YOU FINALLY SEE THE LIGHT...
IF THE COUNSELOR DIES, THEN SO DO YOU!
HURRY IT UP!!
RIGHT.
SNIP SNIP
ARTERIAL BLEEDING'S PRETTY BAD. HE'S IN SHOCK FROM LOW BLOOD PRESSURE.
I CAN APPLY PRESSURE WITH MY HAND TO STOP THE BLEEDING...

...BUT I NEED TO SUTURE THE SKIN!! GET ME SOME NEEDLE AND THREAD! EVEN A STAPLER WILL DO!

O-OKAY!!

HURRY!!

A STAPLER?

GASP!

CLAMP

THERE!

CLAMP

CLAMP

WH-WHAT ARE YOU DOING?

HUH?

UMPH!

I'VE DONE WHAT I CAN. NOW HE NEEDS TO GET TO A HOSPITAL!

51

WHAT ARE YOU THINKING?! YOU WANT TO DIE?!

A HOSPITAL?!

SHOOT ME IF YOU WANT!

THEN *YOU* TAKE HIM TO THE HOSPITAL!

!!

DAMN.

ZA

THE POLICE!!

!!
PUT ME... DOWN ...
SAVE YOURSELF.
I JUST REALIZED ...
I *THOUGHT* I KNEW YOU...YOU'RE THE DOCTOR WANTED FOR THE SERIAL MURDERS...
.....
PUT ME DOWN.
LISTEN, I'M NO INDIS-CRIMINATE KILLER...
I ONLY KILLED THE PRESIDENT OF GWE AND HIS BODY-GUARDS.
NO ONE ELSE WAS KILLED?
!!
THERE WAS...THE GIRL AT THE STORE...

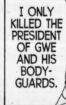

SO YOU KNEW...
YOU SHOT AND KILLED THAT GIRL...
WHY DID YOU HELP ME...?
I COULD TELL BY THE LOOK IN YOUR EYES...
YOU WEREN'T AFRAID OF GETTING SHOT...
WH-WHY DID YOU HELP A TERRORIST LIKE ME...?

BECAUSE I BELIEVE IN YOU...
I BELIEVE IN YOUR HUMANITY.
GO!
THE POLICE ARE ALMOST HERE!
YOU HANG IN THERE...
RUSTLE
YOU'RE ...
YOU'RE A GREAT DOCTOR...

WHERE'S THE MONEY?!
YOU DIDN'T FIX HIM UP AND LEAVE WITHOUT GETTING PAID, DID YOU?!
THE SUSPECTS IN THE ERFURT STATION INCIDENT HAVE BEEN ARRESTED.
THE TWO SUSPECTS SURRENDERED QUIETLY...
......
HEY!! WE AIN'T OPERATING NO CHARITY OUTFIT HERE!!

WELL, WELL...THIS IS AN EXCELLENT PLACE.
IT'S ONLY A TWENTY-MINUTE DRIVE TO THE CENTER OF BERLIN. VERY CONVENIENT AND IT'S A NICE NEIGHBORHOOD.
AN EXECUTIVE OF GERLACH ELECTRONICS JUST MOVED OUT OF HERE TWO MONTHS AGO.
IT'S A RARE PROPERTY FOR THE EAST SIDE.
WASN'T THIS THE RESIDENCE OF MR. LIEBERT-- THE FORMER HEAD OF COMMERCE OF EAST GERMANY?
HUH?
W-WELL, I DON'T KNOW ALL THE DETAILS, BUT IT WAS BUILT FOR SOMEONE OF IMPORTANCE. IT HAS A STRONG FOUNDATION.
PLEASE, COME IN!
Chapter 3 511 Kinderheim

Former East Berlin
Chapter 3
511 Kinderheim

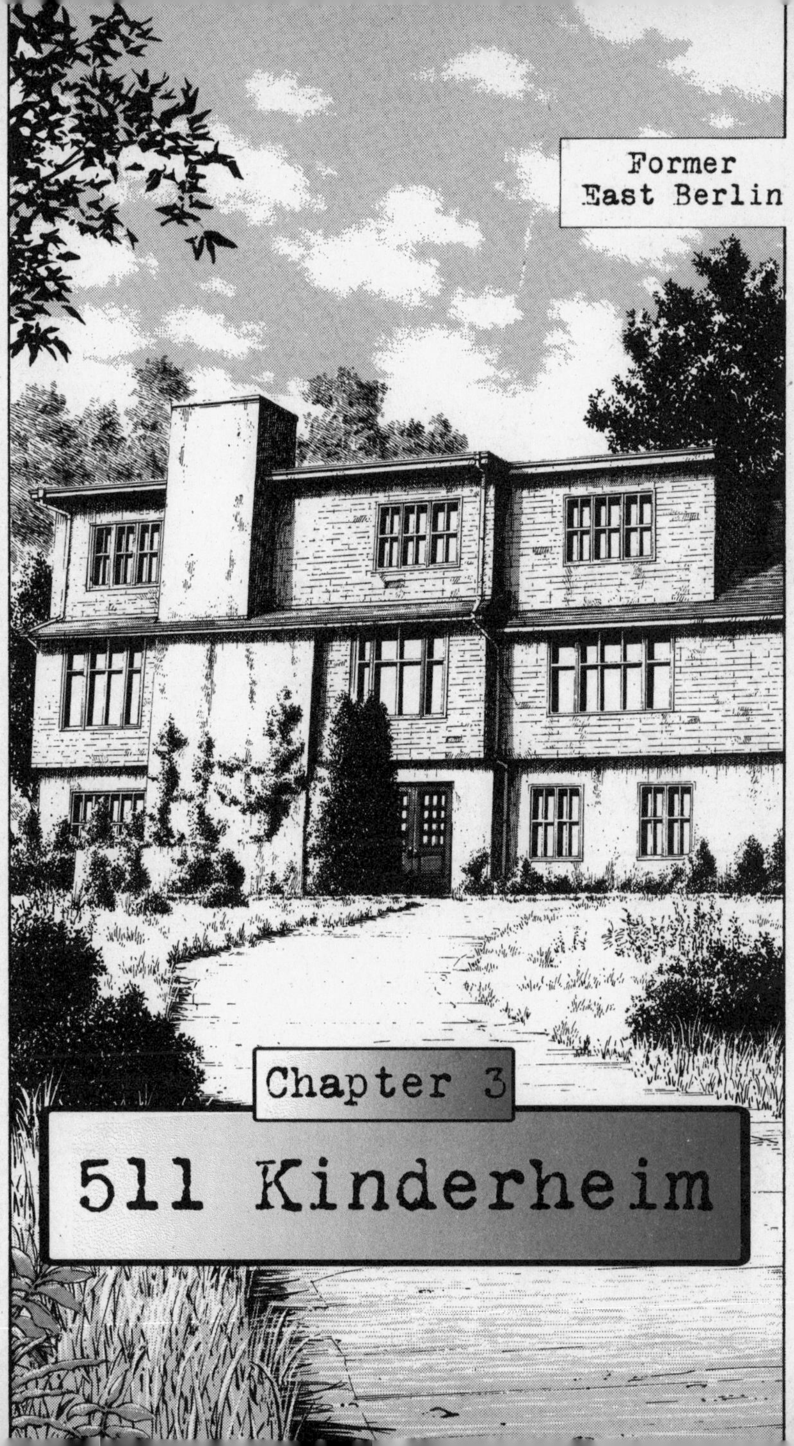

WHAT?
YOU'RE HERE TO FIND INFORMATION ON LIEBERT?
YOU'RE NOT A BUYER?!
SORRY. I JUST NEED THE INFORMATION.
I DON'T KNOW ANYTHING.
HE ADOPTED TWINS DURING THE TIME HE WAS HERE.
I TOLD YOU, I DON'T KNOW ANYTHING.
WHO OWNS THIS PROPERTY NOW?
LISTEN, A LOT OF PROPERTY IN EAST GERMANY USED TO BE OWNED BY JEWS WHO HAD TO FLEE DURING THE NAZI REGIME.
IN SOME CASES, THE EAST GERMAN GOVERNMENT ENDED UP BORROWING LAND FROM PEOPLE ON THE WEST SIDE OR EVEN PEOPLE IN OTHER COUNTRIES.
BESIDES, OUR COMPANY ONLY ENTERED THE EASTERN MARKET AFTER THE WALL FELL. WE DON'T KNOW MUCH ABOUT OLD STORIES!
...
HURRY UP, THEN. I'M LOCKING UP.
...

COULD THERE POSSIBLY BE SOMEONE AROUND WHO KNEW THE LIEBERTS?
SIGH ...
LIKE I SAID, HIGH-RANKING OFFICIALS LIVED IN THIS NEIGHBOR-HOOD.
THEY ALL FLED AFTER THE WALL FELL-- ESPECIALLY PEOPLE FROM THE MINISTRY OF THE INTERIOR...
WAIT ...
?
ACTUALLY, I DO RECALL AN EX-OFFICIAL WHO LIVES ABOUT TEN HOUSES DOWN THE ROAD.
...YES, I REMEMBER LIEBERT.
IF ONLY HE'D HAVE WAITED UNTIL AFTER EAST GERMANY FELL...
HE FLED ONLY TO BE KILLED...
DID HE HAVE TWINS-- A BOY AND GIRL?!

TWINS ...?
YES, THAT'S RIGHT...
HE ADOPTED THEM FROM AN ORPHANAGE...
AN ORPHAN-AGE?
THEY WERE CUTE. HE ALWAYS WANTED KIDS.
WHICH ORPHAN-AGE WAS IT?!
YES, *UMM...*
I BELIEVE IT WAS 511 KINDERHEIM.
...

...
THEY'RE GOING TO TURN IT INTO A SUPER-MARKET.
THANK GOODNESS WE'RE RID OF THIS CREEPY PLACE.

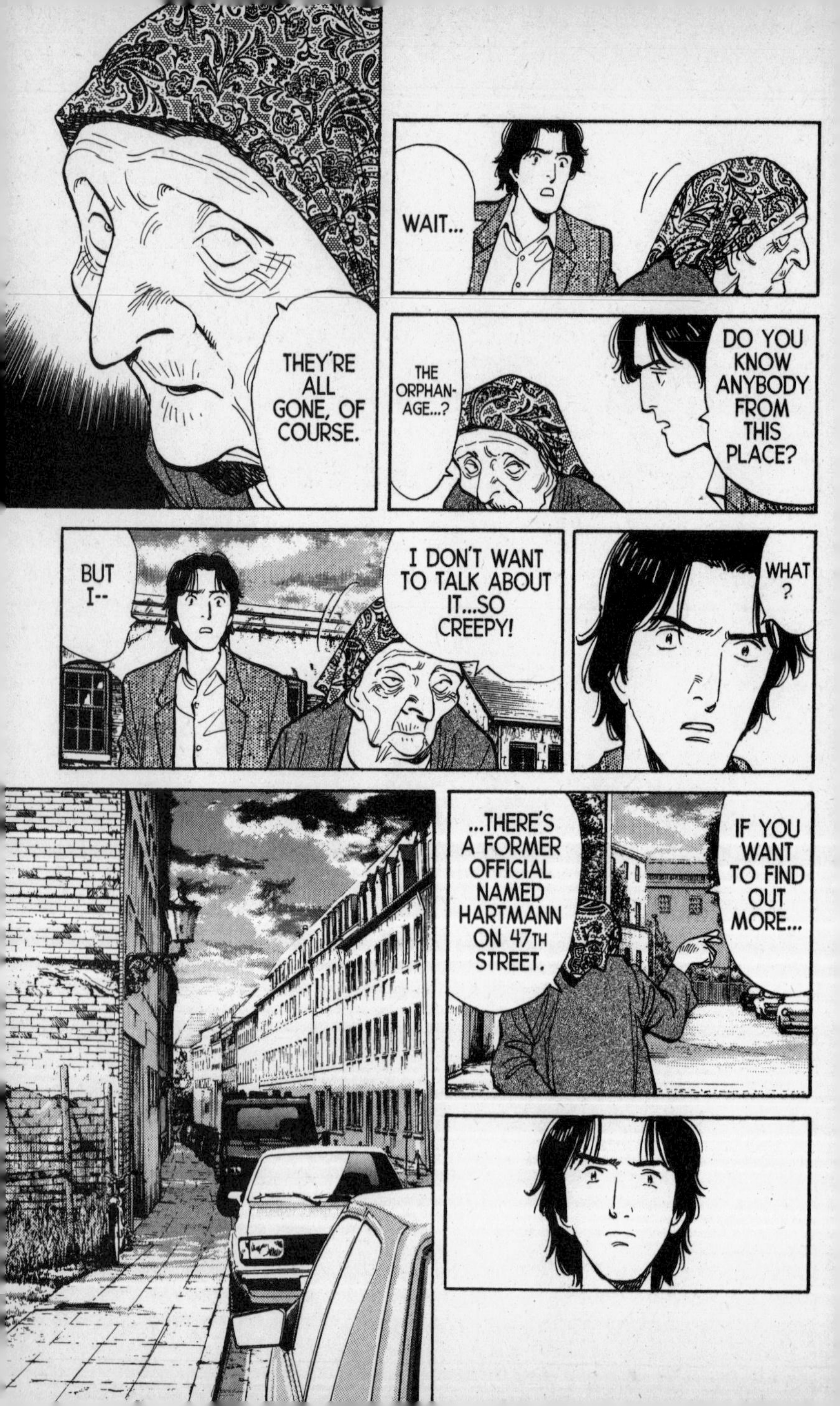
WAIT...
DO YOU KNOW ANYBODY FROM THIS PLACE?
THE ORPHANAGE...?
THEY'RE ALL GONE, OF COURSE.
WHAT?
I DON'T WANT TO TALK ABOUT IT...SO CREEPY!
BUT I--
IF YOU WANT TO FIND OUT MORE...
...THERE'S A FORMER OFFICIAL NAMED HARTMANN ON 47TH STREET.

HELLO THERE. DO YOU KNOW IF A MAN NAMED HARTMANN LIVES AROUND HERE?

?

...

HEY!!

IT'S OKAY. DON'T BE AFRAID.

LET ME SEE.

YOU'RE HURT!

THIS WILL STING. BUT IT'LL HELP YOU GET BETTER.

IT'S INFECTED.

OKAY, THAT'S IT.

CAREFUL, DON'T TRIP!!

HEY...

TP TP

65

HART-
MANN...

BUZZ
BUZZ

Hartmann

WIRTH

FOSTER
PARENT
...?

AFTER
EAST
GERMANY
FELL, I
BECAME
THEIR
FOSTER
PARENT.

...

66

YES, UNTIL THEY WERE ADOPTED OR OTHERWISE GOT SET UP.
THE BOY IN THE MIDDLE WAS ADOPTED BY A COMPANY PRESIDENT...
THE ONE ON THE LEFT ENLISTED IN THE ARMY.
AND I STILL HAVE ONE LEFT.
IT MUST BE HARD WORK FOR YOU.
I WOULDN'T CALL IT WORK...
AS A DISTRICT OFFICIAL FOR THE MINISTRY OF WELFARE, I WAS AGAINST THE WAY THE GOVERNMENT HANDLED THEM.
AFTER THE FALL OF SOCIALISM, I TRIED DOING THINGS MY WAY.
OF COURSE, I DON'T HAVE MANY RE- SOURCES, AND IT ISN'T EASY.

BUT IT'S FAR BETTER THAN BEING IN THAT ORPHANAGE.
.....
THE MINISTRY OF THE INTERIOR AND THE MINISTRY OF WELFARE RAN 511 KINDERHEIM AS A SPECIAL ORPHAN-AGE.
OF COURSE, NO ORPHANAGE DURING THAT TIME WAS A GREAT PLACE TO BE...
BUT THESE SPECIAL ORPHANAGES WERE PARTICULARLY NOTORIOUS. CHILDREN OF CRIMINALS, POLITICAL PRISONERS, AND DEFECTORS WERE SENT TO THESE FACILITIES.
DISCRIMINATION AND INHUMANE CRUELTY WERE PART OF EVERYDAY LIFE. THE CHILDREN COULDN'T DO ANYTHING ABOUT IT. IT WAS A CONTRADICTORY CLASH OF SOCIALISM AND TOTALITARIANISM.
...
THE GOVERNMENT CLAIMED THEY WERE REEDUCATING THE ORPHANS TO BE MODEL CITIZENS, BUT IN ACTUALITY THEY WERE TREATED AS CRIMINALS. THE DIRECTOR AND INSTRUCTORS WERE TERRIBLE.
THE WORST OF THE BUNCH STOLE CARE PACKAGES SENT FOR THESE CHILDREN AND SOLD THEM FOR PERSONAL PROFIT. *THEY* WERE THE REAL CRIMINALS.

FEAR AND VIOLENCE CONTROLLED THESE PLACES.
YOU CAN'T RAISE NORMAL PEOPLE THAT WAY.
THEN IT HAPPENED ...
WHAT ?
WHAT HAPPENED ?
YOU ASKED ME ABOUT THE TWINS?
!!
THE TWINS ?
YOU KNOW SOME-THING ABOUT THEM?
I BELIEVE THE GIRL WAS IN ANOTHER ORPHANAGE.
BUT I REMEMBER THE BOY-- JOHAN.
JOHAN ...
YES! TELL ME ABOUT JOHAN.

?
...
I-IT WAS TOP SECRET. THE GOVERNMENT PLACED A STRICT GAG ON IT.
SHAKE SHAKE
WHAT HAPPENED?
IT'S IN THE PAST NOW...
I DON'T MIND TALKING ABOUT THE INCIDENT...
INCIDENT?!
WHAT INCIDENT?!
WHAT DID JOHAN DO?
WHAT HAPPENED?

A REVOLUTION...

?

HEY!

DIETER, COME SAY HELLO TO OUR GUEST.

!!

I'M HOME.

71

DIETER, WHERE ARE YOUR MANNERS?
IT'S OKAY!
WE MET EARLIER.
RIGHT?
PLEASE, CONTINUE. I'D LIKE TO HEAR MORE.
NO, NOT IN FRONT OF THE CHILD.
I UNDERSTAND.
AND IT'S GETTING LATE. I SHOULD BE--
?
PULL
DIETER!
PERHAPS YOU SHOULD STAY FOR DINNER.
SURE.

DOES THAT MEAN YOU'LL WRITE AN ARTICLE ABOUT WHAT WE WERE TALKING ABOUT?

MR. TENMA, YOU SAID YOU'RE A FREELANCE JOURNALIST...

CLNK CLANK

KLATTA

THAT'S RIGHT...

Y-YES...

A CHILD'S FUTURE DEPENDS ON THE ADULTS THAT RAISE HIM.

THEN PLEASE EMPHASIZE THIS--

DREAMS...?

IF WE DO, THEN THEY'LL BE ABLE TO HAVE WONDERFUL DREAMS.

WE MUST SHOW THE CHILDREN THE RIGHT PATH.

DIETER, WHAT ARE *YOUR* DREAMS?

73

I WANT A SOCCER BALL!

SOCCER BALL...

WHAT?

...

I SEE.

I'LL BE BACK. I'LL CALL AGAIN TOMORROW.

I'M SORRY WE DIDN'T FINISH OUR DISCUSSION...

THANK YOU FOR DINNER.

KTNK

74

BUMP

BUMP

KNOCK KNOCK

IT'S KENZO TENMA!

MR. HART-MANN!

MR. HARTMANN! WHAT'S WRONG?! MR HARTMANN!!

AHHHHH!

!!

MR. HART-MANN !!
M-MR. TENMA!!
A!!
WHAT HAPPENED ?!
HE WAS PLAYING AROUND AND FELL OFF THE CHAIR...*OH,* DIETER!!
ARGHH!
NNGH!

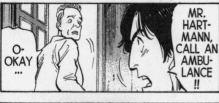

WHERE DOES IT HURT?
NNGH!
MR. HART-MANN, CALL AN AMBU-LANCE !!
O-OKAY ...
LET'S SEE.
?!
WH-WHAT ARE ALL THESE BRUISES ?!

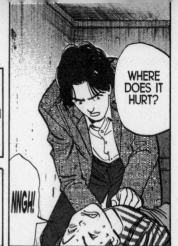

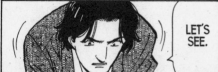

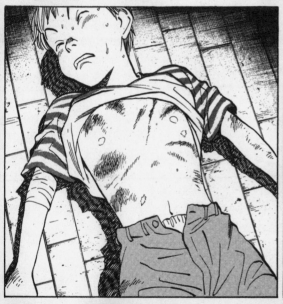

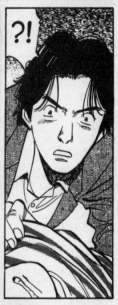

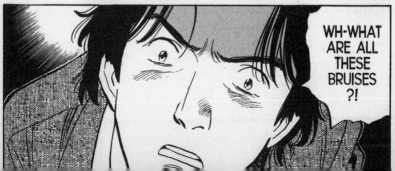

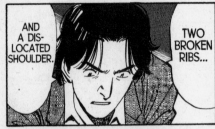

DOES THIS HURT?
AHHHH!!
TWO BROKEN RIBS...
AND A DIS-LOCATED SHOULDER.
FROM FALLING OFF A CHAIR?
THE AMBULANCE WILL BE HERE SOON. EVERYTHING'S GOING TO BE FINE.
RIGHT...
BUT HOW DID HE GET ALL THESE BRUISES?
EVERY-THING'S FINE. YOU CAN GO NOW.
THE WAY YOU USE YOUR HANDS...
...JUST LIKE A DOCTOR.
UH... NO.

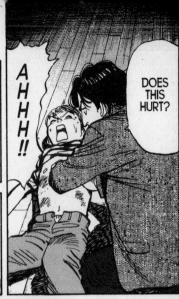

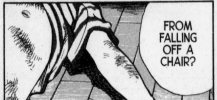

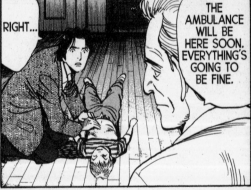

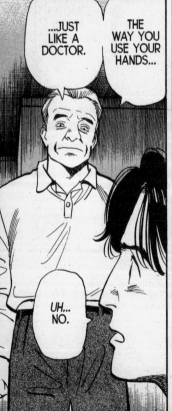

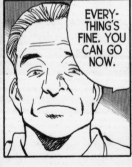

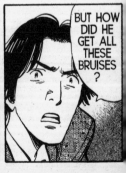

TENMA... I'VE HEARD THAT NAME BEFORE...
YOU'RE A DOCTOR, AREN'T YOU?
THE ONE WANTED FOR MURDER!!
...

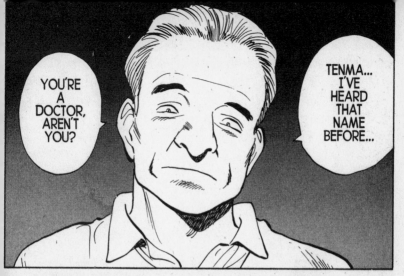

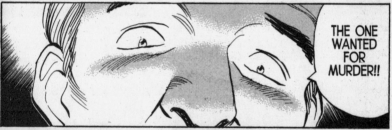

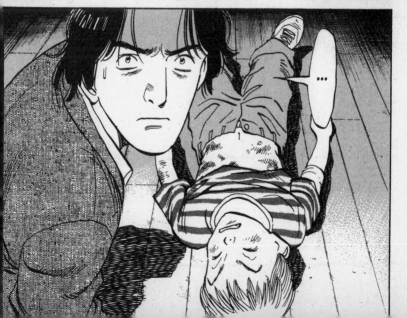

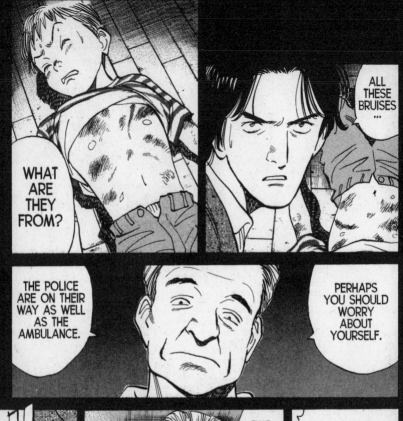

ALL THESE BRUISES ...
WHAT ARE THEY FROM?
PERHAPS YOU SHOULD WORRY ABOUT YOURSELF.
THE POLICE ARE ON THEIR WAY AS WELL AS THE AMBULANCE.
MR. HARTMANN, WHAT REALLY HAPPENED TO DIETER?!
THAT SHOULDN'T CONCERN THE LIKES OF YOU.
YOU'RE WANTED FOR MURDER.

Chapter 4
Project

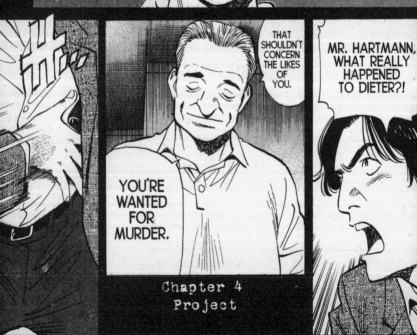

Chapter 4

Project

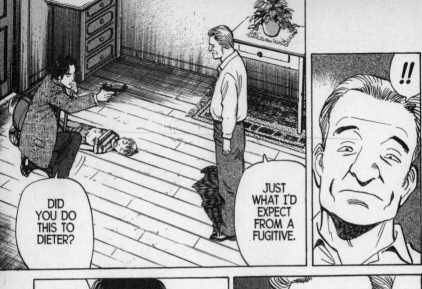

!!
JUST WHAT I'D EXPECT FROM A FUGITIVE.
DID YOU DO THIS TO DIETER?
ME?
DO WHAT?
YOU'RE ABUSING DIETER.
ABUSING?
I'D DO NO SUCH THING.
RIGHT, DIETER?
NNGH...

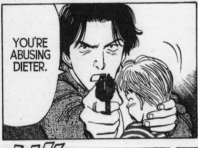

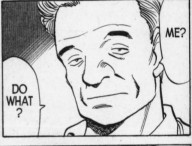

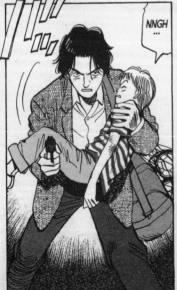

WHAT ARE YOU DOING?

TAKING HIM TO THE HOSPITAL.

FIRST MURDER, NOW KIDNAPPING?

DON'T MOVE!!

SHUF

THE POLICE WILL CATCH YOU.

CREAK

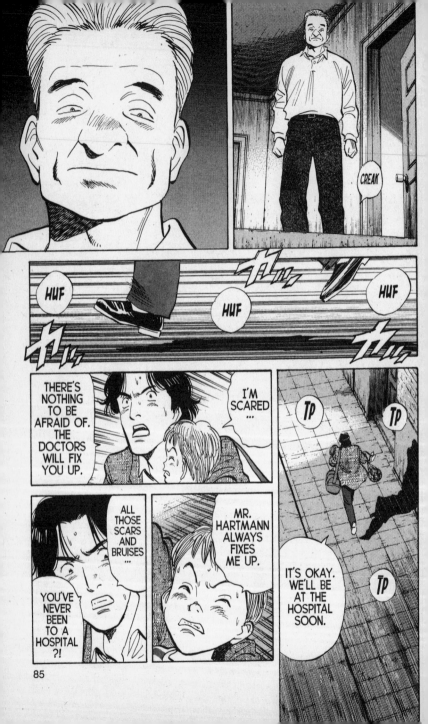

CREAK
HUF
HUF
HUF
TP
TP
IT'S OKAY. WE'LL BE AT THE HOSPITAL SOON.
TP
I'M SCARED ...
THERE'S NOTHING TO BE AFRAID OF. THE DOCTORS WILL FIX YOU UP.
MR. HARTMANN ALWAYS FIXES ME UP.
ALL THOSE SCARS AND BRUISES ...
YOU'VE NEVER BEEN TO A HOSPITAL ?!

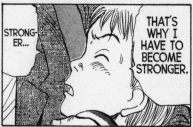

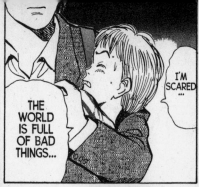

I'M SCARED...
THE WORLD IS FULL OF BAD THINGS...
THAT'S WHY I HAVE TO BECOME STRONGER.
STRONG-ER...
IS THAT WHAT HE TOLD YOU?!
THE WORLD... IS DARK...
THE FUTURE... IS DARK...
...
THAT'S NOT TRUE!
...
THE WORLD ISN'T DARK. THAT'S A LIE!

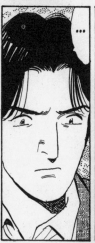

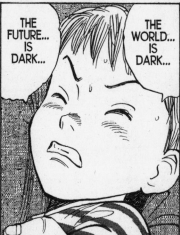

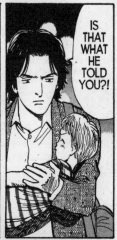

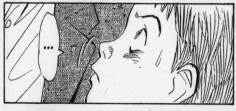

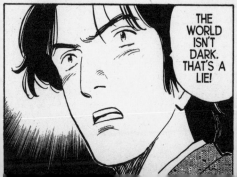

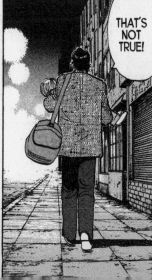

OH, I ALMOST FORGOT. THIS SOCCER BALL'S FOR YOU.

REALLY?

!!

YES, REALLY.

WOW!

TOMORROW WILL BE A GOOD DAY.

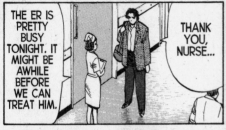

THANK YOU, NURSE...
THE ER IS PRETTY BUSY TONIGHT. IT MIGHT BE AWHILE BEFORE WE CAN TREAT HIM.
P-PLEASE DO WHAT YOU CAN...
THERE WAS A BIG ACCI-DENT...
THE DRIVER OF THE BUS DIED INSTANTLY. WE'LL NEED TO QUESTION THE TRUCK DRIVER.
HE BROKE BOTH HIS LEGS BUT HE CAN STILL TALK, RIGHT?
TREATMENT FIRST! QUESTIONS LATER!!
!!
FINE, WE'LL BE WAITING.
...
I'LL BE BACK IN TWO HOURS. PLEASE TAKE CARE OF THE BOY.
...?

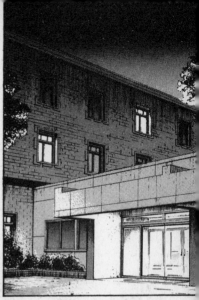

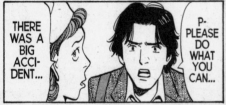

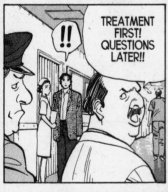

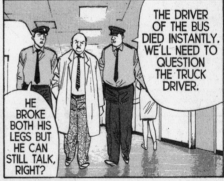

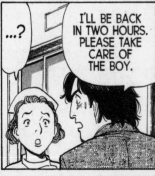

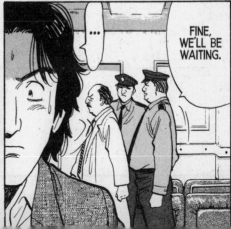

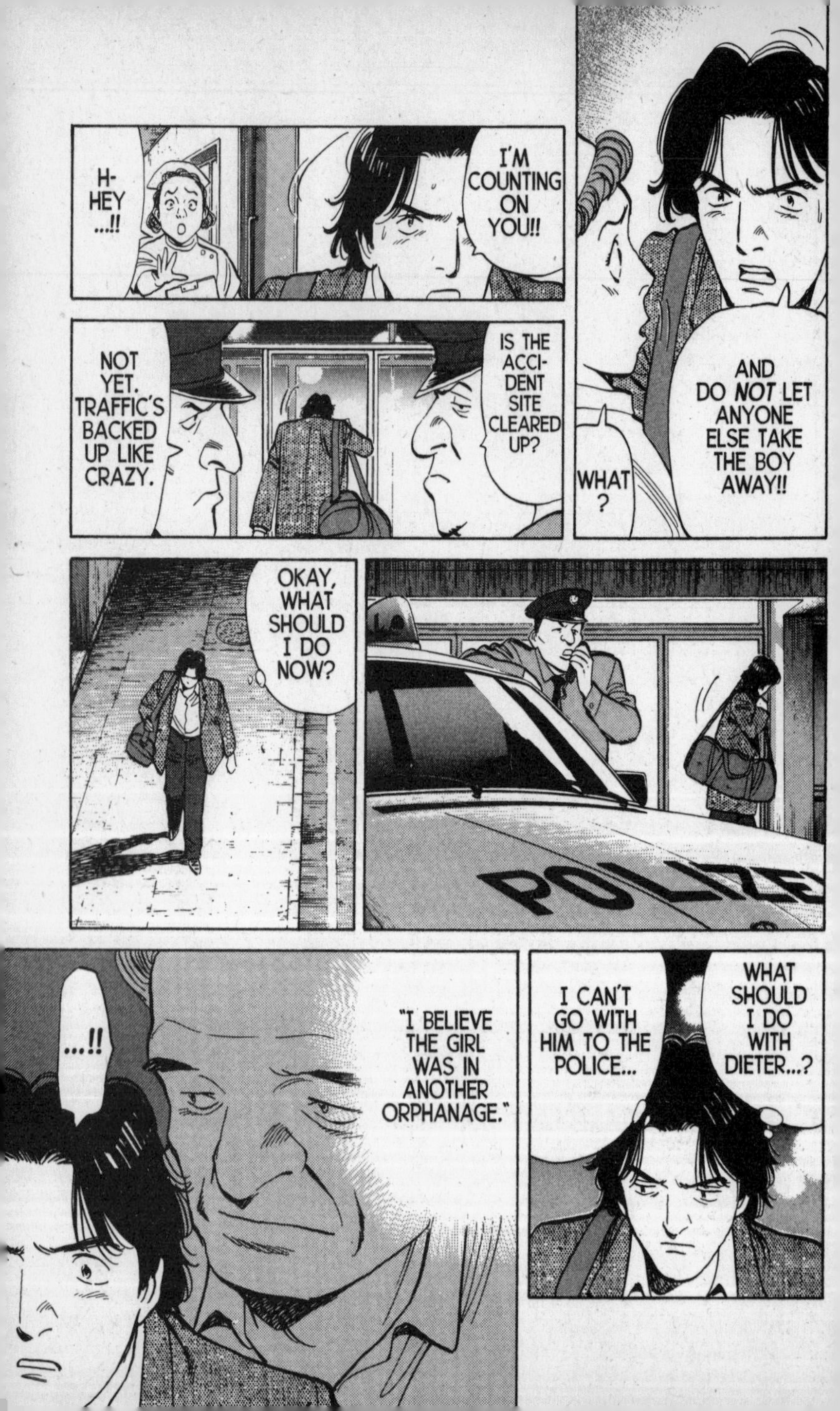

AND DO *NOT* LET ANYONE ELSE TAKE THE BOY AWAY!!
WHAT?
I'M COUNTING ON YOU!!
H-HEY ...!!
IS THE ACCIDENT SITE CLEARED UP?
NOT YET. TRAFFIC'S BACKED UP LIKE CRAZY.
POLIZE
OKAY, WHAT SHOULD I DO NOW?
WHAT SHOULD I DO WITH DIETER...?
I CAN'T GO WITH HIM TO THE POLICE...
"I BELIEVE THE GIRL WAS IN ANOTHER ORPHANAGE."
...!!

THAT'S IT!!

EXCUSE ME, IS THERE AN ORPHANAGE AROUND HERE?

AN ORPHANAGE...?

SHUF

WHO ARE YOU?! WHAT ARE YOU DOING COMING HERE AT THIS HOUR?

I'M SORRY, BUT THIS CHILD NEEDS YOU...

YOU WANT ME TO TAKE A BOY IN?

WELL... I...

...BUT IF I DON'T KNOW WHO YOU ARE...

I UNDERSTAND HE'S BEING ABUSED...

DID ANNA LIEBERT LIVE HERE?

I CAN'T TAKE IN A CHILD FROM A SUSPICIOUS PERSON WHO WON'T EVEN IDENTIFY HIMSELF.

W-WAIT...

ANNA... LIEBERT?

SO ANNA DID STAY HERE!!

I...

YOU KNOW ANNA LIEBERT?

SHE GOES TO HEIDELBERG UNIVERSITY...

REALLY! SO SHE'S DOING WELL!!

HOW'S ANNA? IS SHE DOING WELL?

OF COURSE I KNEW ANNA...

Y-YES...

JOHAN...

WHAT WAS THE BOY'S NAME...?

I KNEW SHE AND HER TWIN BROTHER WERE ADOPTED BY MR. LIEBERT OF THE COMMERCE MINISTRY...

ANNA WAS A NICE GIRL...

THEY WERE REALLY CLOSE. I FELT SORRY FOR THEM WHEN THEY HAD TO BE SEPARATED.

JOHAN, THAT'S IT!!

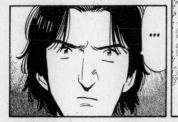

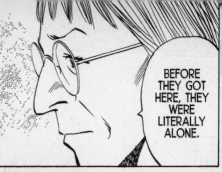

BEFORE THEY GOT HERE, THEY WERE LITERALLY ALONE.
...
THEY WERE FOUND WALKING HAND IN HAND NEAR THE BORDER OF CZECHOSLOVAKIA. IT WAS JUST THE TWO OF THEM SHIVERING IN THE COLD.
...
MR. LIEBERT WAS ONLY GOING TO ADOPT JOHAN...
...BUT JOHAN WOULDN'T GO WITHOUT HIS SISTER. ANNA MADE IT TO THE OTHER SIDE BECAUSE OF HER BROTHER.
I HEARD ORPHANAGES ON THE EAST SIDE WERE TERRIBLE...
!!

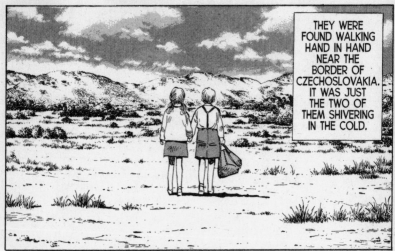

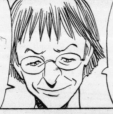

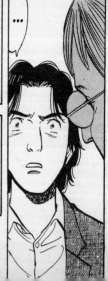

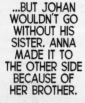

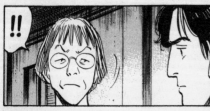

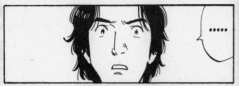

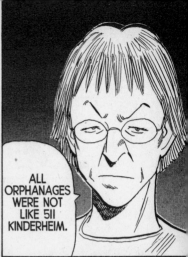

ALL ORPHANAGES WERE NOT LIKE 511 KINDERHEIM.
......
THUNK
INGE, THE BATH-ROOM'S THE OTHER WAY.
MAMA...
IT'S OKAY. DON'T BE SCARED.
YOU'RE A BIG GIRL NOW. YOU CAN GO ALL BY YOURSELF, RIGHT?
YES...
CREAK

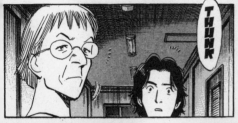

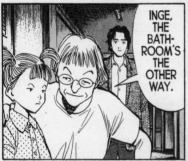

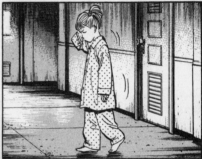

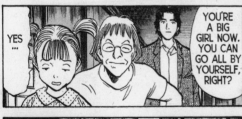

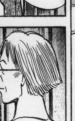

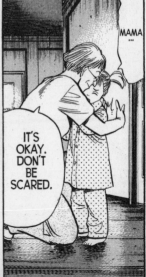

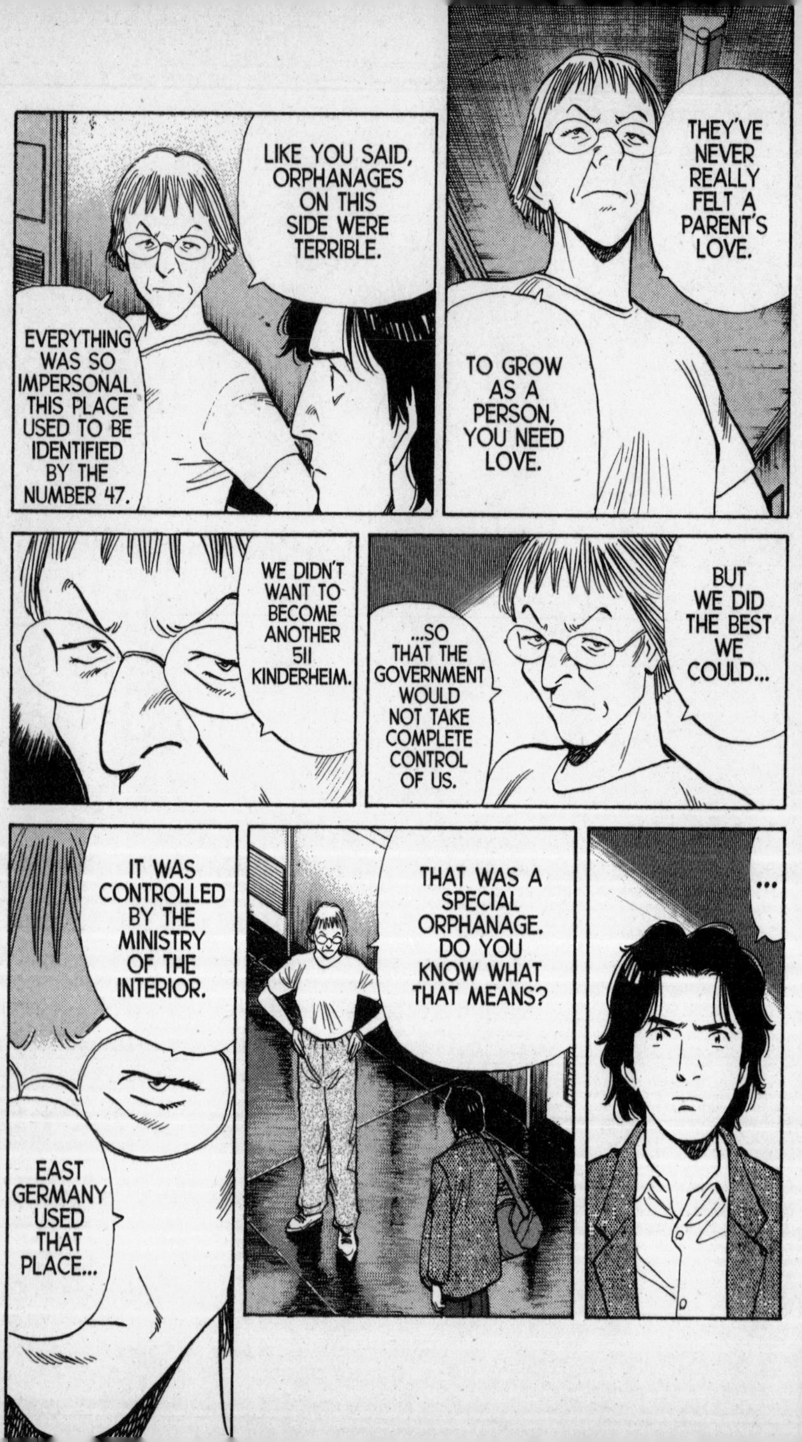
THEY'VE NEVER REALLY FELT A PARENT'S LOVE.
TO GROW AS A PERSON, YOU NEED LOVE.
LIKE YOU SAID, ORPHANAGES ON THIS SIDE WERE TERRIBLE.
EVERYTHING WAS SO IMPERSONAL. THIS PLACE USED TO BE IDENTIFIED BY THE NUMBER 47.
BUT WE DID THE BEST WE COULD...
...SO THAT THE GOVERNMENT WOULD NOT TAKE COMPLETE CONTROL OF US.
WE DIDN'T WANT TO BECOME ANOTHER 511 KINDERHEIM.
...
THAT WAS A SPECIAL ORPHANAGE. DO YOU KNOW WHAT THAT MEANS?
IT WAS CONTROLLED BY THE MINISTRY OF THE INTERIOR.
EAST GERMANY USED THAT PLACE...

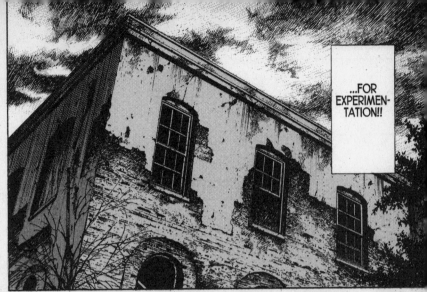

...FOR EXPERIMENTATION!!
WHAT ?!
THEY RAN A PROJECT TO TURN CHILDREN INTO PERFECT SOLDIERS...
THE MENTAL STATE AND ENTIRE PERSONA OF THE CHILDREN WERE EXPERIMENTALLY RECONSTRUCTED. THEY HAD CHILDREN FORM FACTIONS AND OBSERVED THE AGGRESSIVE FIGHTING AND HATE THAT RESULTED.
IT WAS AN EXPERIMENT TO CREATE ICE-COLD HUMANS WITH ABSOLUTELY NO SENSE OF COMPASSION.

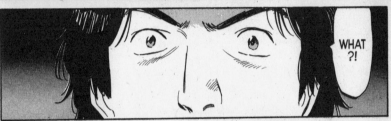

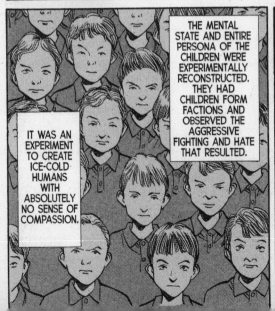

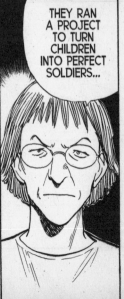

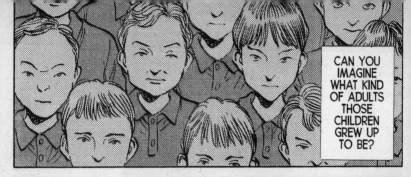

CAN YOU IMAGINE WHAT KIND OF ADULTS THOSE CHILDREN GREW UP TO BE?
...
BUT NOW THERE'S NO WAY TO PROVE THAT ANYTHING LIKE THAT EVER WENT ON THERE.
ALL THOSE TYPES OF SECRET DOCUMENTS WERE BURNED BEFORE THE WALL FELL.
EVERYONE WHO HAD ANYTHING TO DO WITH THE PRO-JECT HAS FLED THE COUNTRY.
...
BUT I'VE HEARD RUMORS...
THERE'S ONE OFFICIAL WHO MANAGED TO REMAIN HERE.
?
HE WAS INVOLVED WITH THAT EVIL 511 KINDERHEIM PROJECT.
ALTHOUGH HE WAS ACTUALLY A PEDIATRIC PSYCHOLOGIST FOR THE MINISTRY OF THE INTERIOR POLICE...
...HIS OFFICIAL TITLE WAS THAT OF A DISTRICT OFFICIAL.

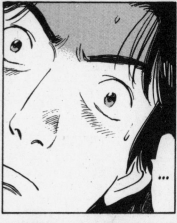

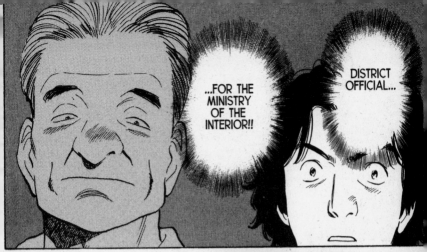

DISTRICT OFFICIAL...
...FOR THE MINISTRY OF THE INTERIOR!!
INGE, ARE YOU ALL DONE?
SWEET DREAMS.
GOOD NIGHT.
KTNK
GOOD NIGHT.
BUT EVERYTHING WAS COVERED UP-- ESPECIALLY AFTER THAT INCIDENT.
INCIDENT?

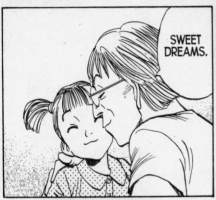

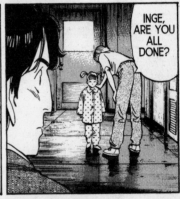

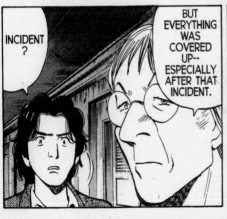

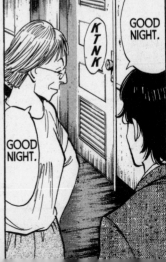

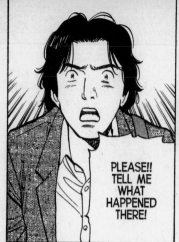

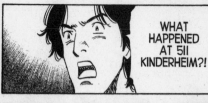

WHAT HAPPENED AT 5II KINDERHEIM?!
I'VE SAID TOO MUCH. TOO MANY BAD MEMORIES THERE...
PLEASE!! TELL ME WHAT HAPPENED THERE!
...
THE SOCCER BALL...?
WHAT?
WHERE'S MY SOCCER BALL?
OH...

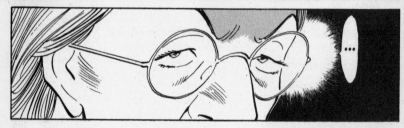

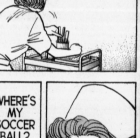

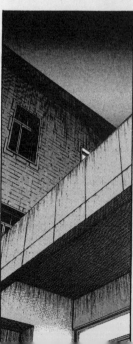

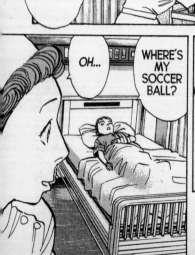

HERE YOU GO.

BUT YOU CAN'T PLAY UNTIL YOU GET BETTER.

KLNK

THAT MAN WILL BE BACK TO PICK YOU UP SOON. YOU JUST GET SOME REST UNTIL HE DOES.

I DON'T KNOW WHAT REALLY HAPPENED.

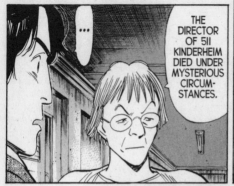

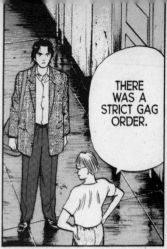

THERE WAS A STRICT GAG ORDER.
THE DIRECTOR OF 511 KINDERHEIM DIED UNDER MYSTERIOUS CIRCUM-STANCES.
...
THEN THE INSTRUCTORS STARTED FIGHTING OVER THE DIRECTOR'S SEAT.
IT WAS COMPLETE CHAOS. THEY COULDN'T EVEN CONTROL THE CHILDREN.
IT'S A MIRACLE JOHAN CAME OUT ALIVE.
WHAT EXACTLY HAPPENED AT 511 KINDERHEIM?
EVERYONE DIED.
WHAT?!

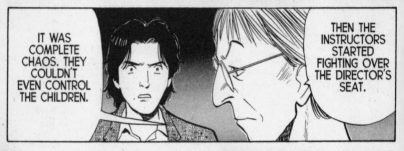

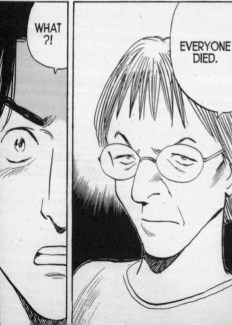

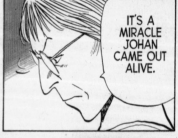

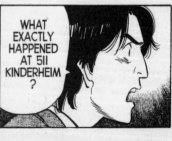

EVERYONE
DIED. THE
INSTRUCTORS,
THE STUDENTS--
THEY ALL
KILLED EACH
OTHER.

22

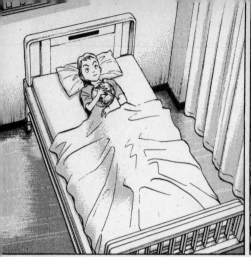

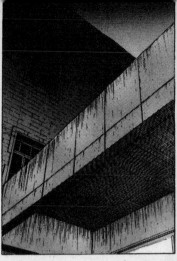

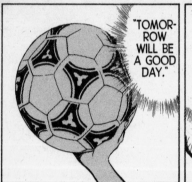

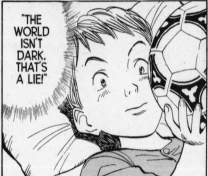

"THE WORLD ISN'T DARK. THAT'S A LIE!"
"TOMOR-ROW WILL BE A GOOD DAY."
...
DIETER ...
GATHER UP YOUR THINGS.

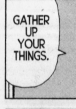

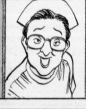

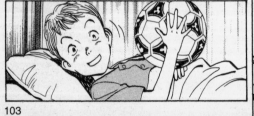

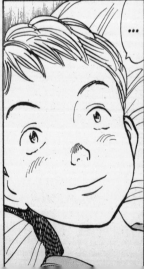

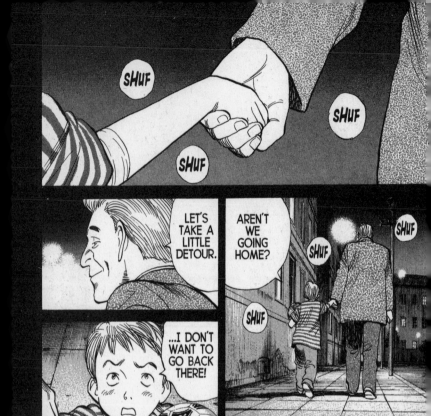

SHUF
SHUF
SHUF
SHUF
AREN'T WE GOING HOME?
SHUF
SHUF
LET'S TAKE A LITTLE DETOUR.
...I DON'T WANT TO GO BACK THERE!
...
NO!! NO!!
DIETER ...

Chapter 5
A Little Experiment

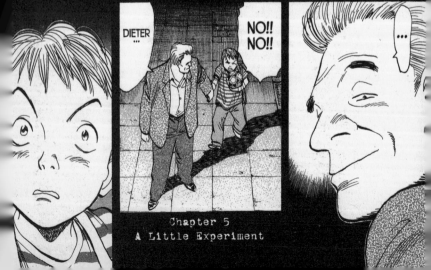

DIETER, BE A GOOD BOY.

Chapter 5
A Little Experiment

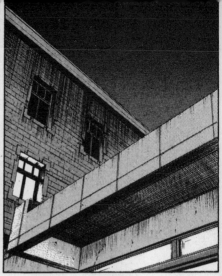

WHAT ?!
I TOLD YOU NOT TO LET HIM GO WITH ANYONE ELSE!!
B-BUT...
HE WAS HIS FOSTER PARENT.
AND HE WAS A GENTLEMAN-- UNLIKE YOU!
N-NO, BUT THAT MAN IS--
AND THE BOY...
...WAS HAPPY TO GO WITH HIM.

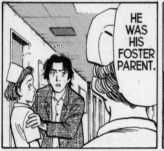

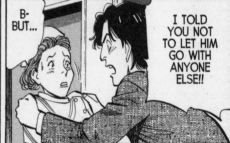

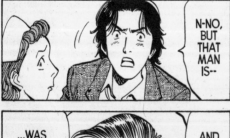

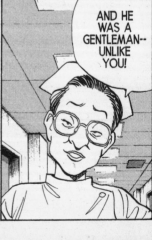

DIETER !
HUF
HUF
TMP
TMP
TMP
HUF
HUF
HUF
KLK

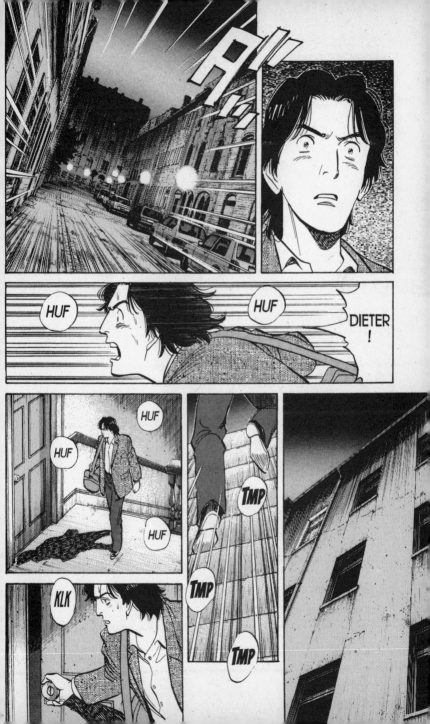

DIETER!!

THEY'RE NOT BACK YET.

DIETER?

CREAK

CREAK

HART-MANN'S LIBRARY.

WHERE
IS IT?!

THESE
PHOTOS--
THEY'RE
ALL OF THE
SAME
PLACE.

GASP
!!

110

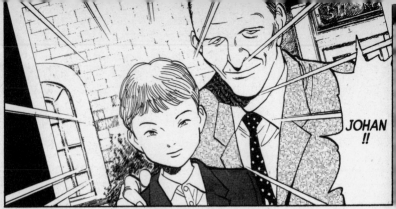

JOHAN !!
WHO'S THE MAN NEXT TO HIM?
!!
THESE WERE ALL TAKEN AT 5II KINDERHEIM.
OVER TEN YEARS AGO...
"EVERYONE DIED. THE INSTRUCTORS, THE STUDENTS-- THEY ALL KILLED EACH OTHER."
...
COULD DIETER BE AN-OTHER--?!

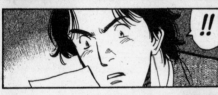

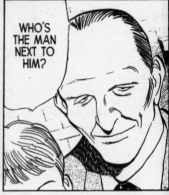

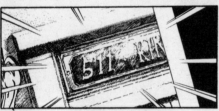

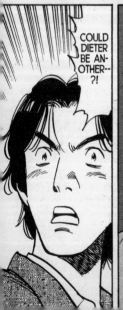

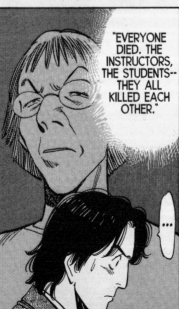

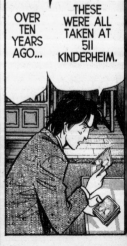

SHUF

SHUF

!!

SHUF

BUMP
BUMP
TMP
!!
DIETER!!

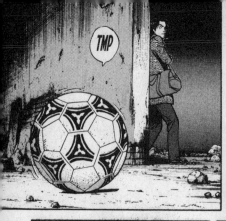

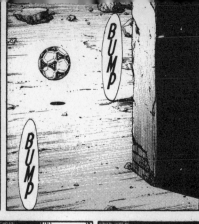

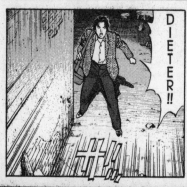

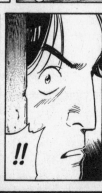

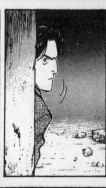

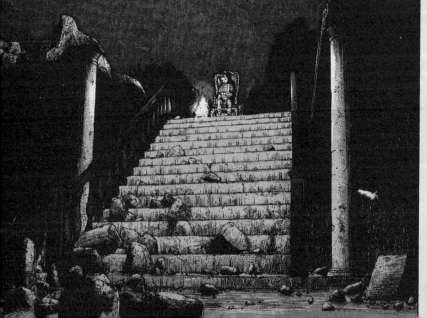

DIETER! I'M COMING.

KRKL KRKL

!!

HART-MANN!

LURK

HE CAN'T SEE...

HE CAN'T SEE WHAT JOHAN SAW.

HE CAN'T...

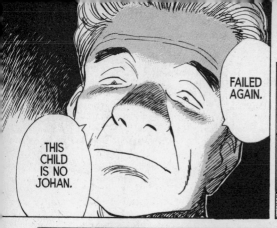

IT'S NO GOOD.
FAILED AGAIN.
THIS CHILD IS NO JOHAN.
...
EVERYONE... EVERYONE DIED.
...
TEN YEARS AGO, THE INSTRUCTORS, THE ORPHANS-- FIFTY PEOPLE DIED.
JOHAN SAT HERE, WATCHING IT ALL.
HE SAW EVERY-THING.

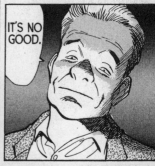

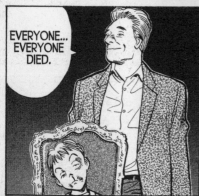

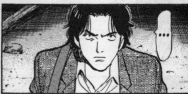

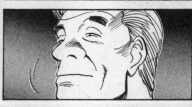

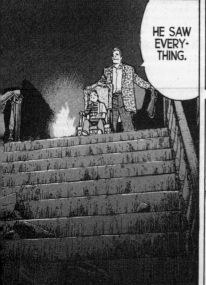

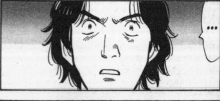

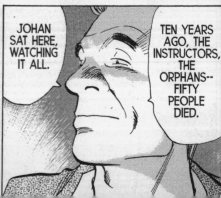

JOHAN JUST SAT AND OBSERVED...

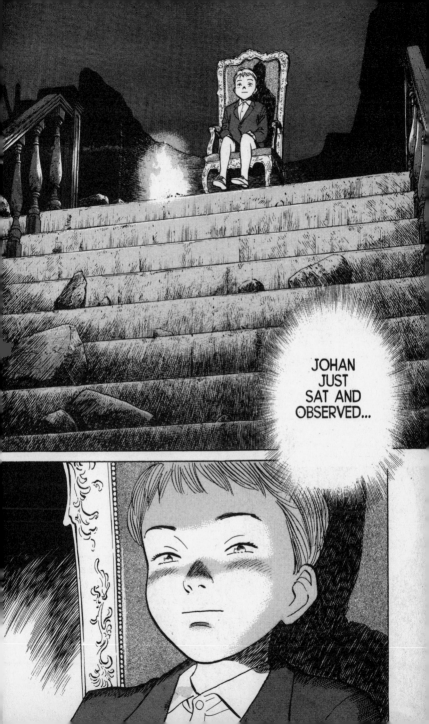

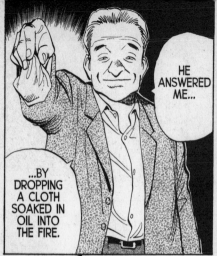

...
I ASKED JOHAN...
I ASKED HIM WHAT HE HAD DONE.
HE ANSWERED ME...
...BY DROPPING A CLOTH SOAKED IN OIL INTO THE FIRE.
ボッ
DO YOU GET IT?
...
"I JUST ADDED A LITTLE FUEL...
"...TO THE HATRED BORN WHEN PEOPLE COME TOGETHER."

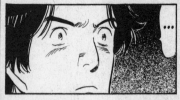

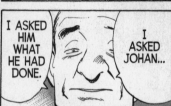

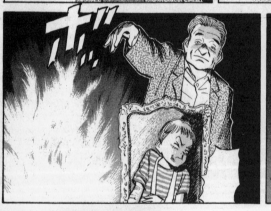

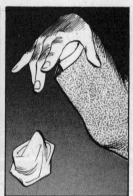

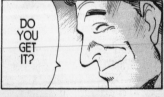

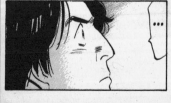

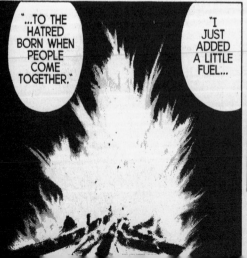

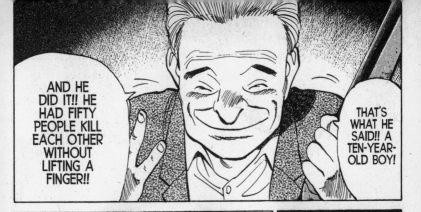

THAT'S WHAT HE SAID!! A TEN-YEAR-OLD BOY!
AND HE DID IT!! HE HAD FIFTY PEOPLE KILL EACH OTHER WITHOUT LIFTING A FINGER!!
...
YOU --!!
YOUR EXPERIMENTS MADE HIM THAT WAY!!
US? NO...
NOT US...
WHAT ...?
IT'S TRUE THAT 511 KINDERHEIM WAS AN EXPERIMENTAL PROJECT TO TRANSFORM ORPHANS INTO PERFECT SOLDIERS...
BUT IT WAS ONLY A LITTLE EXPERIMENT.
...

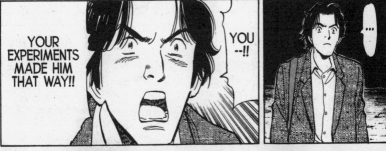

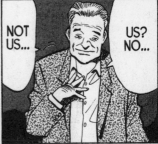

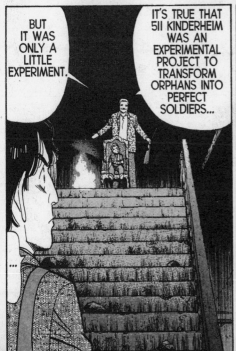

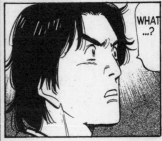

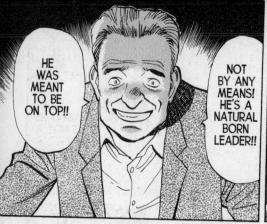

AS FOR JOHAN...
HE'S NO SOLDIER.
NOT BY ANY MEANS! HE'S A NATURAL BORN LEADER!!
HE WAS MEANT TO BE ON TOP!!
THERE'S NO WAY WE COULD HAVE CREATED SUCH A WORK OF ART!
HE WAS BEYOND HUMAN FROM THE START--A MONSTER!
...
JOHAN PREDICTED THAT MAN WOULD ULTIMATELY END UP HATING AND KILLING EACH OTHER TO OBLIVION.
WHAT DO YOU THINK JOHAN'S GOAL WAS?

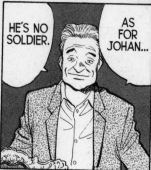

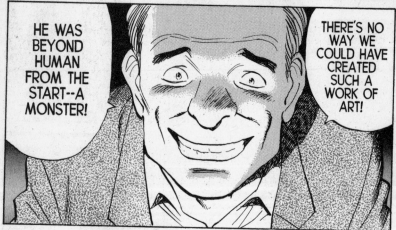

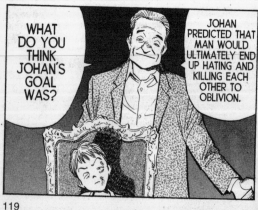

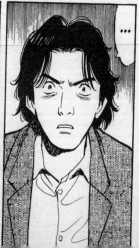

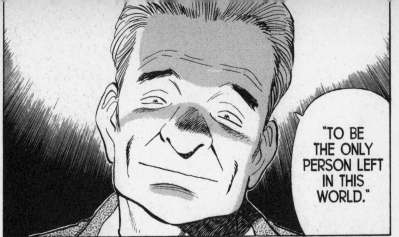

"TO BE THE ONLY PERSON LEFT IN THIS WORLD."
DIETER...
THE FUTURE IS DARK. YOU MUST BECOME MORE LIKE JOHAN...
WHY DO YOU FAIL?
WHY CAN'T YOU BE LIKE JOHAN?!

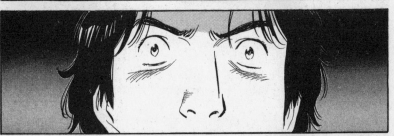

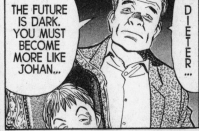

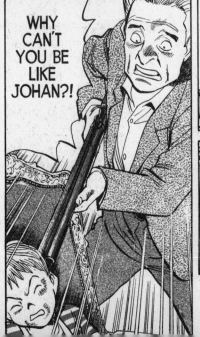

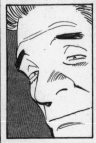

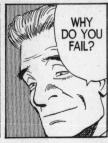

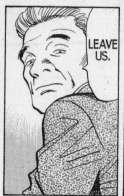

STOP IT!!
IF YOU DON'T, I'LL SHOOT!!
LEAVE US.
THIS IS *OUR* PROBLEM. IT'S NONE OF YOUR BUSINESS!!
DIETER, COME HERE!
...
DR. TENMA, YOU WANT TO KNOW ABOUT JOHAN, RIGHT?
WHAT DO YOU PLAN TO DO?
FIND HIM AND KILL HIM? THAT WILL BE IMPOSSIBLE.

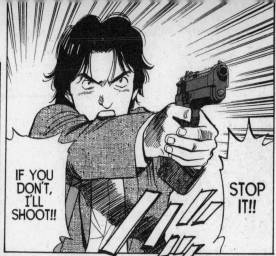

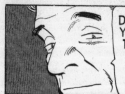

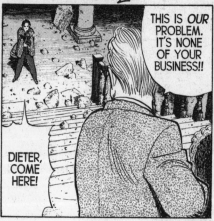

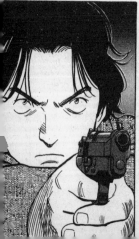

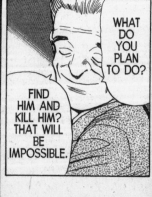

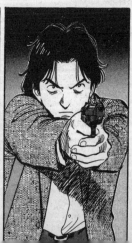

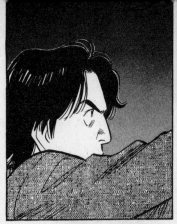

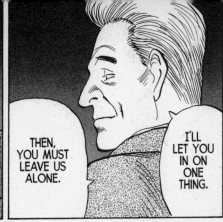

I'LL LET YOU IN ON ONE THING.
THEN, YOU MUST LEAVE US ALONE.
LOOK FOR GENERAL WOLF. HE WAS THE FIRST TO FIND JOHAN AND DISCOVER HIS ABILITIES.
I'M SURE WOLF IS STILL ALIVE.
IS HE THE ONE IN THOSE PHOTOS ?!
THE ONE STANDING NEXT TO JOHAN ...?
WOLF WILL KNOW MORE ABOUT JOHAN.
NOW GO.
DIETER!!
!!
COME WITH ME, OR STAY HERE...
YOU DECIDE FOR YOURSELF!

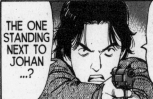

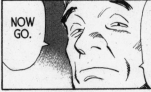

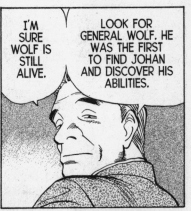

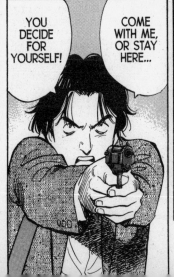

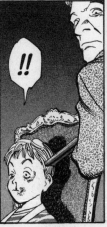

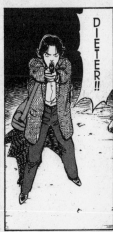

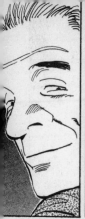

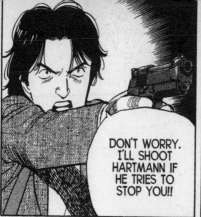

DON'T WORRY. I'LL SHOOT HARTMANN IF HE TRIES TO STOP YOU!!
YOU DECIDE!!
YOU HAVE TO DECIDE!!
YOU CAN'T LIVE WITHOUT ME, DIETER.
YOU'RE *MY* CHILD.

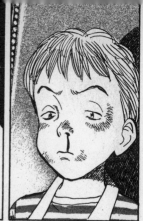

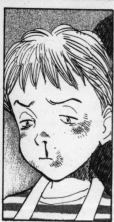

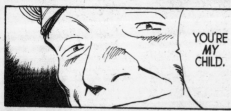

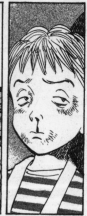

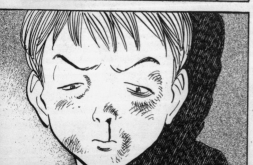

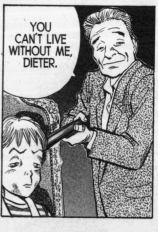

NOW, DR. TENMA, LEAVE US.

IT'S OKAY. COME ON, DIETER...

GOOD.

DIETER...

NO...

COME BACK, MY DEAR DIETER...

DIETER!!

DIETER ...
YOU CAN'T LIVE WITHOUT ME, DIETER!!
STOP!!
MOVE AND I'LL SHOOT!!
I LOVE YOU, DIETER!!
THE WORLD IS DARK. THE FUTURE IS BLEAK!!
TENMA TOLD ME...

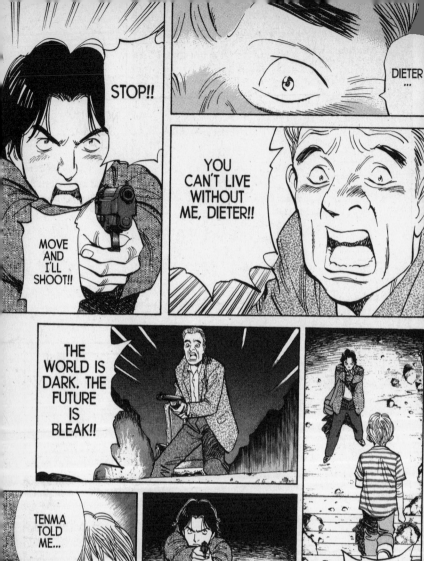

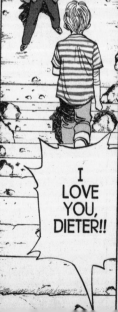

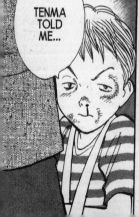

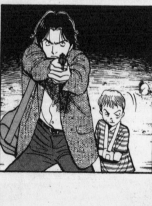

TOMORROW WILL BE A GOOD DAY.
DIETER !!

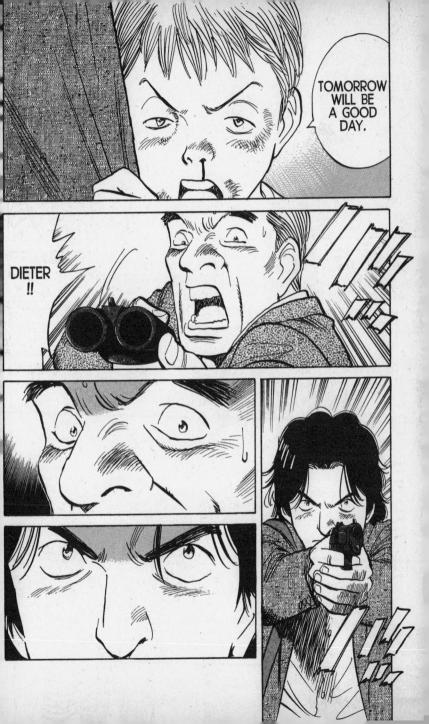

BE BRAVE, DIETER! DON'T BE SCARED!

DIETER !!

DIETER!!!

NO... ARGH...

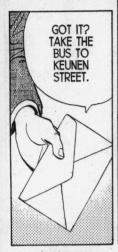

GOT IT? TAKE THE BUS TO KEUNEN STREET.
THE ORPHANAGE IS VERY CLOSE TO THE BUS STOP. GIVE THIS LETTER TO ELNA TYCE.
SHE LOOKS SCARY, BUT SHE'S A REALLY NICE PERSON.
BE A GOOD BOY.
THE BUS WILL BE HERE SOON.

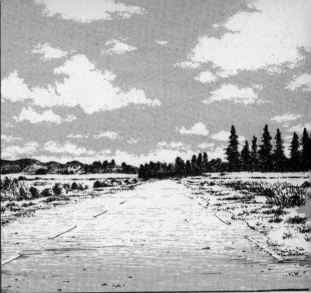

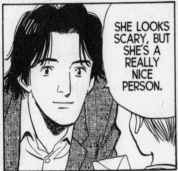

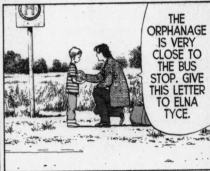

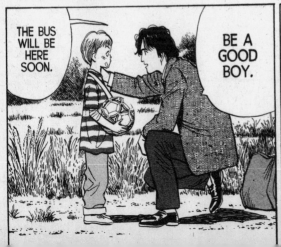

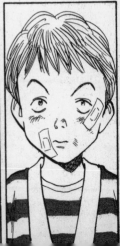

GOODBYE! KEEP UP WITH THE SOCCER PRACTICE.

HERE!!

NO!! YOU CAN'T COME WITH ME!

I'M TELLING YOU...

DIETER!!

YOU CAN'T COME WITH ME...

Chapter 6
Petra and Schumann

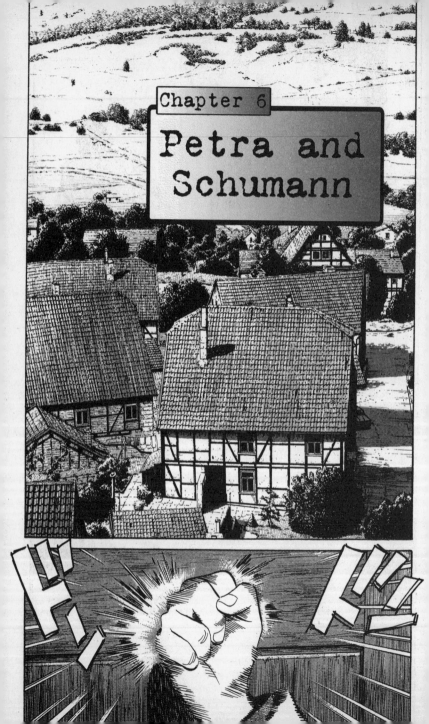

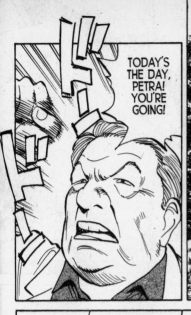

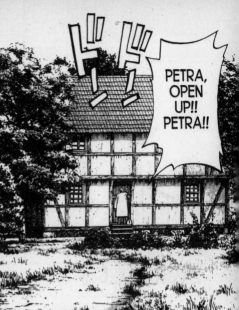

PETRA, OPEN UP!! PETRA!!
TODAY'S THE DAY, PETRA! YOU'RE GOING!
NO, I'M NOT! LEAVE ME ALONE!
I'M NOT LETTING ANY CROOKED DOCTOR TAKE ME ANYWHERE!!
CROOKED?!
WHO DO YOU THINK I'M DOING THIS FOR?!
NOBODY ASKED FOR YOUR HELP!
I WON'T ALLOW A DEVIL LIKE YOU TO OPERATE ON ME!!
WHAT ARE YOU TALKING ABOUT? LET ME EXAMINE YOU!!
HAH! I KNOW YOU KILLED OFF CLARA ZONTAG!!

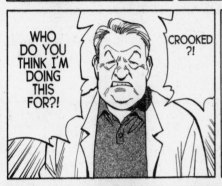

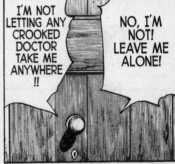

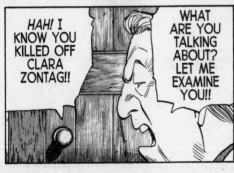

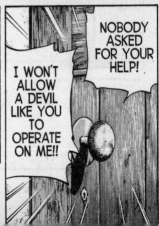

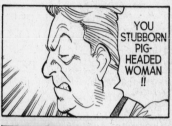

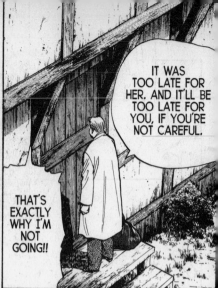

IT WAS TOO LATE FOR HER. AND IT'LL BE TOO LATE FOR YOU, IF YOU'RE NOT CAREFUL.
THAT'S EXACTLY WHY I'M NOT GOING!!
YOU STUBBORN PIG-HEADED WOMAN!!
PIGHEADED WOMAN?! YOU SLASHER!!
I'VE NEVER BEEN TO A DOCTOR AND I'M HEALTHY AS EVER!! NOW LEAVE ME ALONE!!
WHY YOU--
DOC-TOR!!
DOCTOR SCHU-MANN!!
FINK THE DRUNKARD IS AT YOUR CLINIC...
FINK?
HE GOT HIT BY A CAR ON THE HIGHWAY!

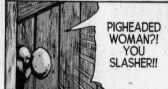

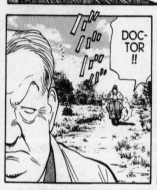

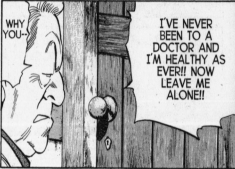

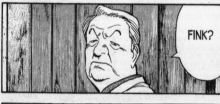

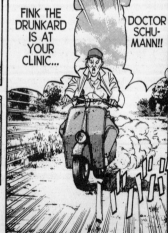

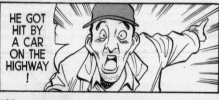

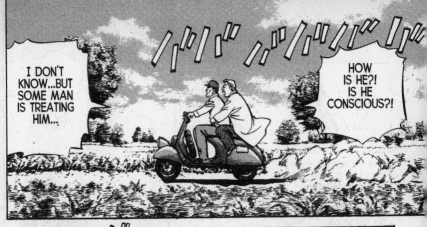

HOW IS HE?! IS HE CONSCIOUS?!
I DON'T KNOW...BUT SOME MAN IS TREATING HIM...
WHAT ?!
SOME GUY WHO WAS JUST PASSING BY...
WHAT ?!
I DON'T KNOW WHO HE IS.

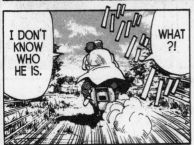

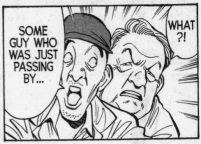

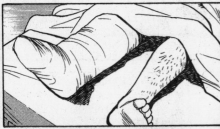

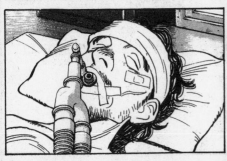

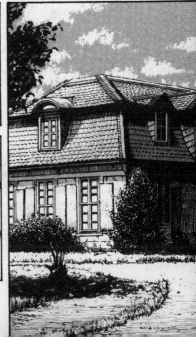

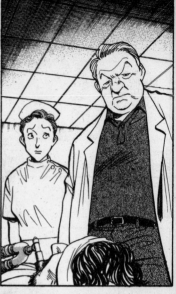

WHAT HAP-PENED?
I SAID YOU WERE OUT, AND HE--
YOU LET A STRANGER TREAT HIM?!
I'M SORRY... I TRIED TO STOP HIM...
...BUT HE SAID HE NEEDED TO SECURE THE AIR PASSAGE TO PREVENT THE PATIENT FROM CHOKING ON HIS OWN VOMIT.
HMPH!
WHO IS HE?!
HE DIS-APPEARED BEFORE I COULD GET HIS NAME.
HE WROTE SOMETHING ON THE PATIENT'S CHART.
HMM... "SUCTIONED VOMIT AND INTUBATED."
HUH?

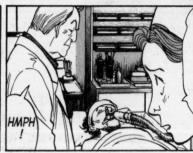

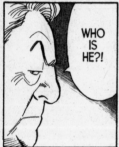

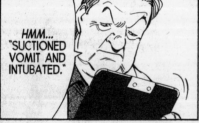

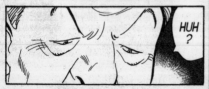

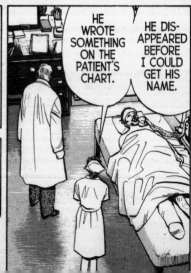

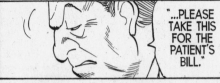

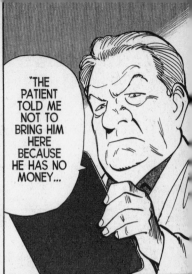

"THE PATIENT TOLD ME NOT TO BRING HIM HERE BECAUSE HE HAS NO MONEY...
"...PLEASE TAKE THIS FOR THE PATIENT'S BILL."
THE BASTARD !!
CRMPL
DOCTOR, WHERE ARE YOU GOING?
I'M GOING TO FIND HIM. WHAT DOES HE LOOK LIKE?!
HE'S AN ASIAN MAN. HE HAD A LITTLE BOY WITH HIM...
BUT WHAT ABOUT MR. FINK?
JUST KEEP HIM IN BED!
BUT THAT MAN ONLY TOOK EMERGENCY MEASURES TO--

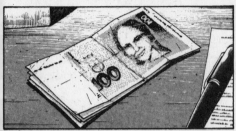

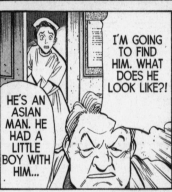

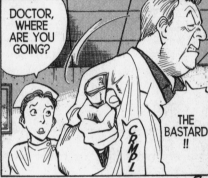

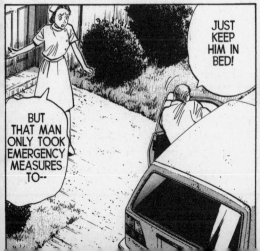

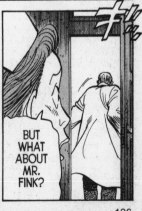

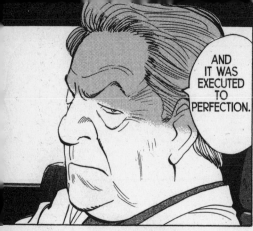

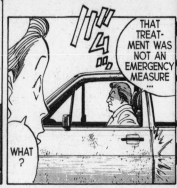

THAT TREAT-MENT WAS NOT AN EMERGENCY MEASURE ...
WHAT ?
AND IT WAS EXECUTED TO PERFECTION.
HEY, DIETER...
...
I REALLY CAN'T TAKE YOU WITH ME...
MNCH MNCH

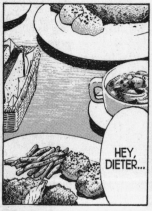

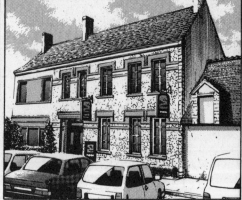

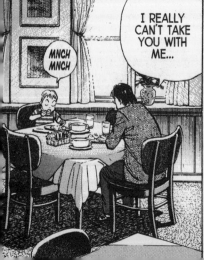

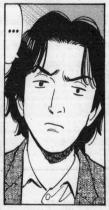

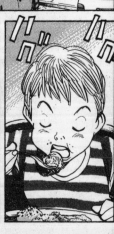

WHAT ABOUT SCHOOL?
YOU WON'T BE ABLE TO GO TO SCHOOL.
CRNCH CRNCH
MNCH MNCH
YOU WON'T MAKE ANY FRIENDS.
YOU CAN'T PLAY SOCCER WITHOUT FRIENDS.
I DO HAVE A FRIEND.
WHO?
CRNCH CRNCH
YOU.
...
LISTEN, DIETER...
WAS IT YOU?

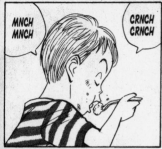

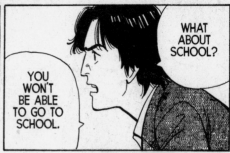

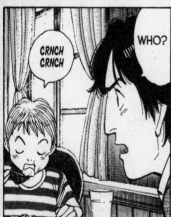

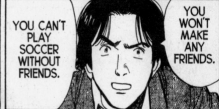

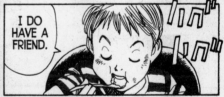

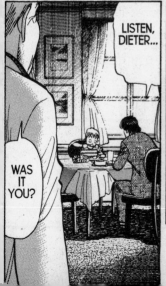

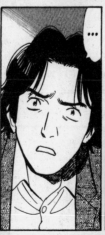

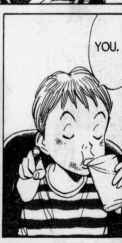

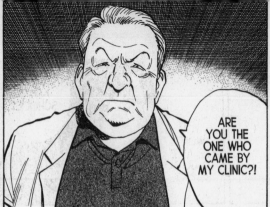

HUH ?
ARE YOU THE ONE WHO CAME BY MY CLINIC?!
DON'T INSULT ME! I DON'T NEED YOUR MONEY!!
!!
I KNOW FINK IS A BROKE ALCOHOLIC.
I WOULDN'T THINK OF CHARGING HIM!
UH...
I... UH...
YOU'RE PROBABLY AN ELITE DOCTOR FROM SOME FANCY HOSPITAL--SMUG WITH SATISFACTION FOR DOING A GOOD DEED.
SLAM
HELLO !
!!

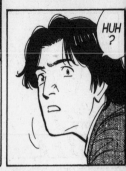

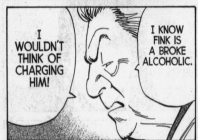

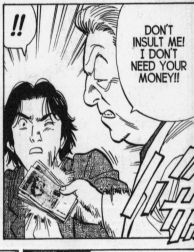

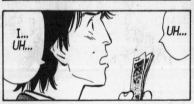

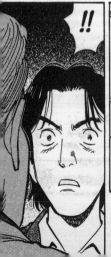

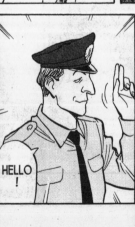

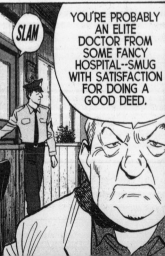

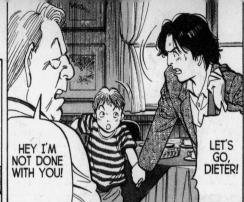

LET'S GO, DIETER!
HEY I'M NOT DONE WITH YOU!
I'M VERY SORRY. I DIDN'T MEAN TO OVERSTEP MY BOUNDS...
SORRY, BUT WE'RE IN A HURRY.
?
I'M LOOKING FOR A WITNESS IN FINK'S HIT-AND-RUN.
...
...
DR. SCHUMANN, HOW'S FINK DOING?
HE'LL BE FINE. I'M MORE WORRIED ABOUT HIS DRINKING.

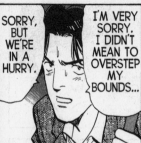

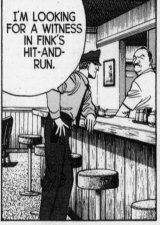

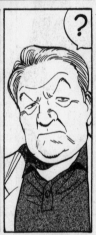

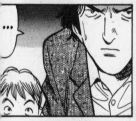

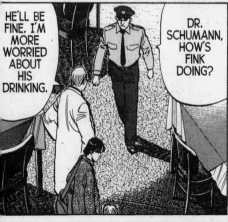

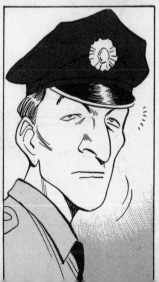

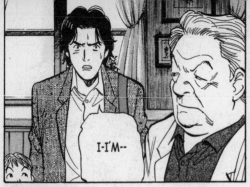

AND YOU ARE ...?
I-I'M--
DR. CHAN, A FRIEND FROM COLLEGE.
HE'S ON VACATION.
?!
DR... CHAN?
HAVE WE MET BEFORE?
...
HE TOOK CARE OF FINK.
WHILE I WAS OUT. WHERE DO YOU THINK *I* WAS?
HUH?
AT YOUR MOTHER'S HOUSE.
MY MOTHER...
TELL HER TO GET LOOKED AT. SHE MIGHT NEED SURGERY.

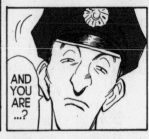

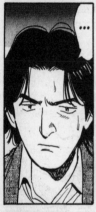

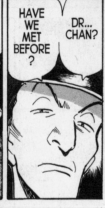

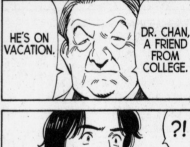

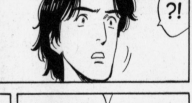

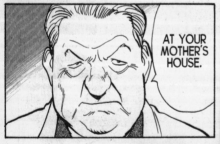

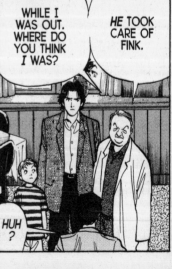

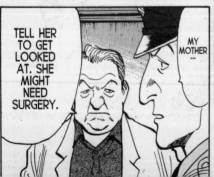

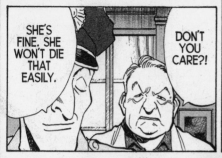

THAT'S IMPOSSIBLE.
SHE'S TOO STUBBORN.
DON'T YOU CARE?!
SHE'S FINE. SHE WON'T DIE THAT EASILY.
WHAT--?!
SHE RAISED ME THIS FAR.
SHE DOESN'T HAVE ANY REGRETS.
WHAT DID YOU SAY?!
PETRA'S STILL GOT PLENTY OF LIVING TO DO!!
WAIT, HEINZ!!
...

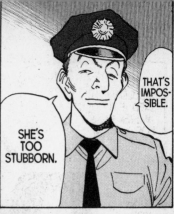

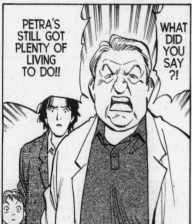

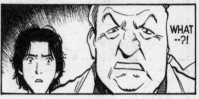

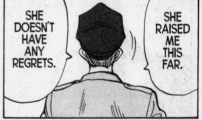

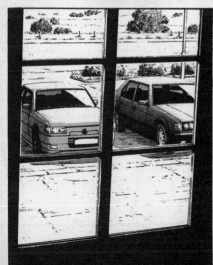

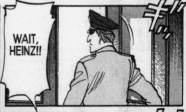

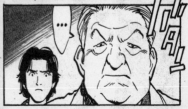

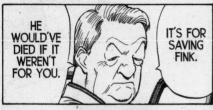

WHY DID YOU LIE?
ABOUT YOU BEING A FRIEND FROM COLLEGE?
IT'S FOR SAVING FINK.
HE WOULD'VE DIED IF IT WEREN'T FOR YOU.
THANK YOU.
YOU TURNED PALE AT THE SIGHT OF HEINZ.
WHAT DID YOU DO?
AT LEAST I KNOW YOU'RE NOT AN ELITE DOCTOR.
THANKS AGAIN. I DON'T KNOW HOW TO REPAY YOU--
REPAY ME?
LET ME BORROW YOU.
HUH?

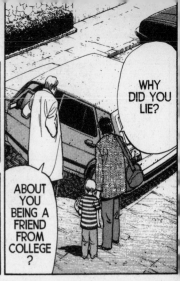

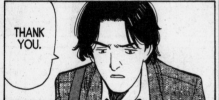

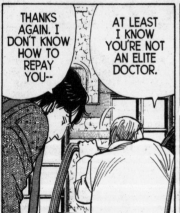

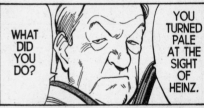

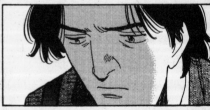

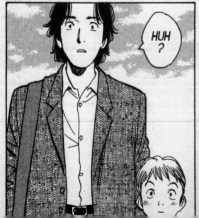

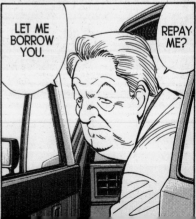

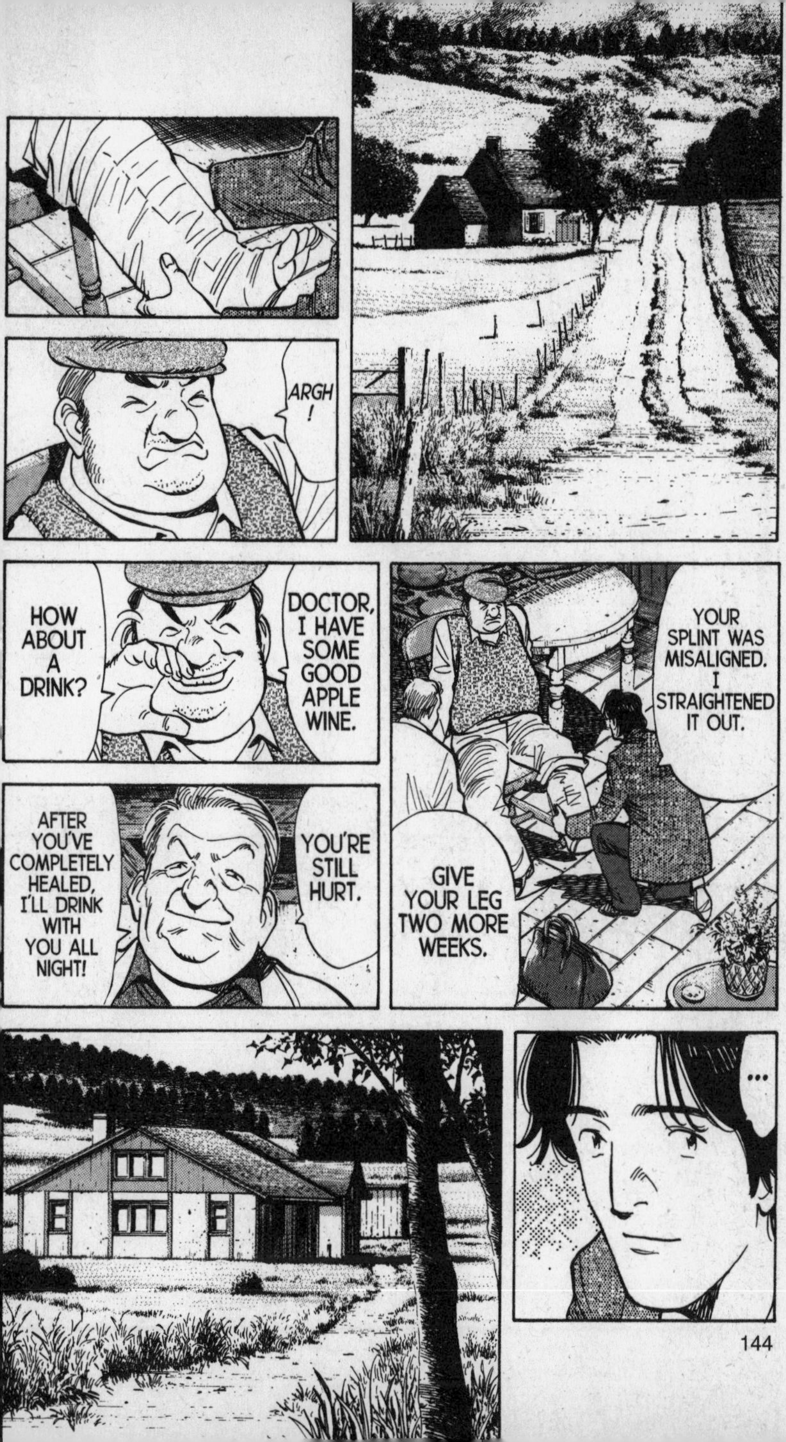
ARGH!
YOUR SPLINT WAS MISALIGNED. I STRAIGHTENED IT OUT.
GIVE YOUR LEG TWO MORE WEEKS.
DOCTOR, I HAVE SOME GOOD APPLE WINE.
HOW ABOUT A DRINK?
YOU'RE STILL HURT.
AFTER YOU'VE COMPLETELY HEALED, I'LL DRINK WITH YOU ALL NIGHT!
...

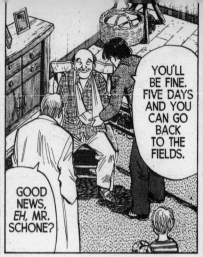

YOU'LL BE FINE. FIVE DAYS AND YOU CAN GO BACK TO THE FIELDS.
GOOD NEWS, *EH,* MR. SCHONE?
DOCTOR, HAVE SOME POTATOES. I GOT A GREAT CROP THIS YEAR!!
I LOVE POTATOES.
I'LL HAVE TO COME BACK AND TAKE A WHOLE TRUCKLOAD! *HA HA HA!*
THANKS FOR THE HELP. I DO WHAT I CAN, BUT MY SPECIALTY IS INTERNAL MEDICINE.
THERE'S ANOTHER TOWN ON THE OTHER SIDE OF THAT MOUNTAIN WHERE I ALSO MAKE ROUNDS...
I'M ONLY ONE MAN AND IT'S HARD TO KEEP UP.
WONDERFUL...
YES. THERE'S NOTHING HERE, BUT IT'S A PEACEFUL PLACE.
NO...I MEAN THAT YOU LOVE ALL THE PEOPLE HERE...
...AND THEY LOVE YOU BACK.

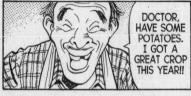

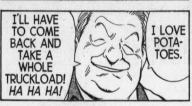

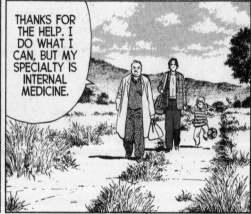

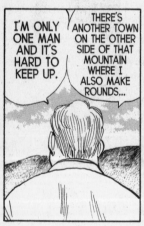

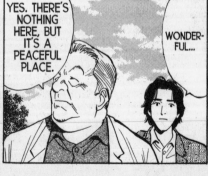

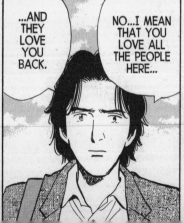

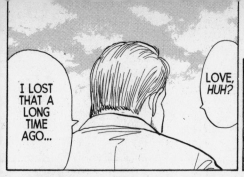

HMPH ...
LOVE, HUH?
I LOST THAT A LONG TIME AGO...
WHAT DO YOU MEAN?
YOU'RE SAVING SO MANY LIVES.
THAT'S WHAT A DOCTOR DOES.
I'M JUST DOING MY JOB.
OKAY, WE'VE GOT ONE MORE HOUSE TO GO. THIS'LL BE A TOUGH ONE!
HUH ?
...
YOU JUST DON'T QUIT, DO YOU?!
NOPE! AND I'LL KEEP COMING BACK!!
...

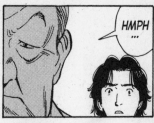

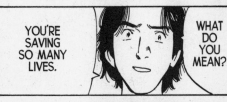

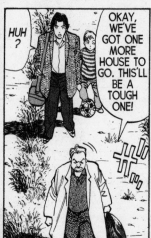

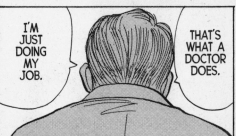

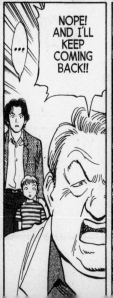

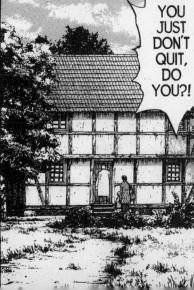

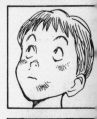

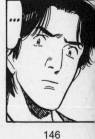

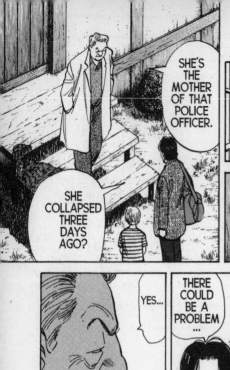

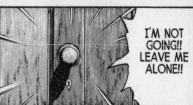

I'M NOT GOING!! LEAVE ME ALONE!!
SHE'S THE MOTHER OF THAT POLICE OFFICER.
SHE COLLAPSED THREE DAYS AGO?
THAT'S RIGHT-- STARTED FEELING ILL OUT IN THE FIELDS. I TRIED TO GET HER TO COME IN TO MY OFFICE, BUT SHE JUST WENT HOME.
THERE COULD BE A PROBLEM ...
YES...
MAY I TRY?
IT WON'T DO ANY GOOD...
ARE YOU STILL OUT THERE?!
I CAN BE WHERE-EVER I WANT!
CALM DOWN. IF YOU YELL, SHE WON'T COME OUT.
I'M GOING TO HAVE YOU CHECKED OUT!! I'M NOT LOSING YOU FROM MY LIFE!!
HUH?

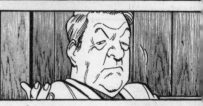

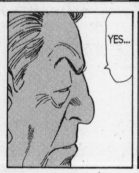

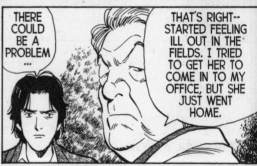

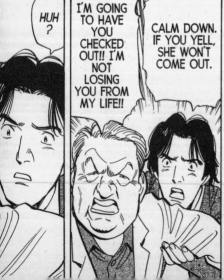

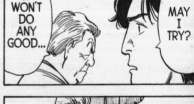

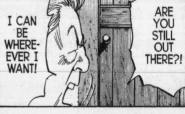

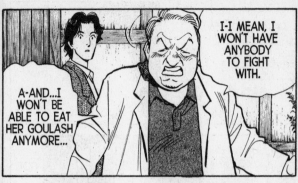

...
I-I MEAN, I WON'T HAVE ANYBODY TO FIGHT WITH.
A-AND...I WON'T BE ABLE TO EAT HER GOULASH ANYMORE...
YOUR FACE IS RED.
WHA--?
WHAT'D YOU SAY, YOU BRAT?!
...
KNOCK KNOCK
MS. PETRA!
PLEASE OPEN THE DOOR!
WHAT NOW? A DIFFERENT DOCTOR?
!!
IT'S NO USE!! A BOMB WON'T EVEN BUDGE THAT DOOR!!

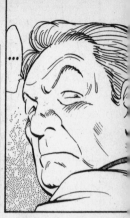

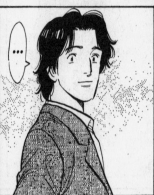

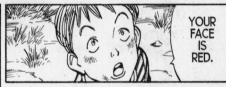

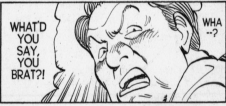

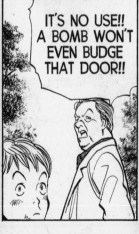

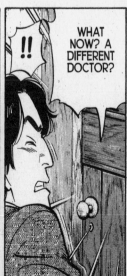

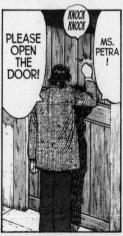

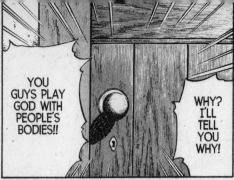

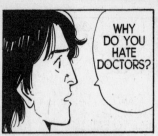

WHY DO YOU HATE DOCTORS?
WHY? I'LL TELL YOU WHY!
YOU GUYS PLAY GOD WITH PEOPLE'S BODIES!!
GOD?
DON'T I WISH...
...
WE TRY OUR BEST, BUT WE MAKE MISTAKES, TOO.
I WISH WE *COULD* BE PERFECT LIKE GOD.
I'M ALWAYS NERVOUS WHEN I LOOK AT PATIENTS.
PLEASE, LET ME JUST SEE YOU.
CREAK

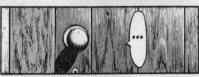

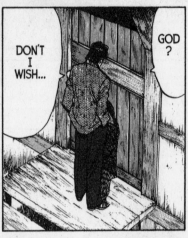

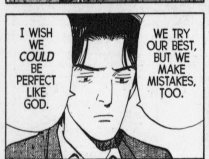

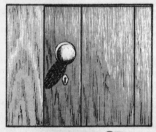

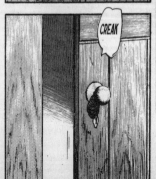

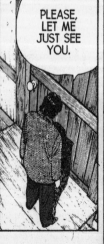

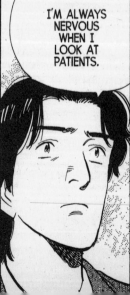

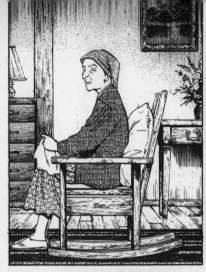

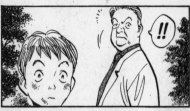

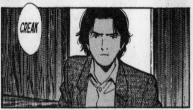

!!
CREAK
ARE YOU MAKING GOULASH?
SNIFF SNIFF
YOU LIKE GOULASH?
YES, AND DR. SCHUMANN *LOVES* YOUR GOULASH.
REALLY ?
GLG GLG
HE'S NEVER TOLD *ME* THAT. I ALWAYS MAKE IT FOR HIM, BUT HE NEVER SAYS ANYTHING.
IF HE LIKES IT, HE SHOULD TELL ME SO!
HE'S SHY.
WOW, THIS LOOKS GOOD!

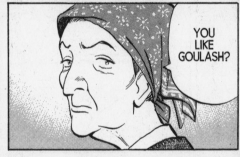

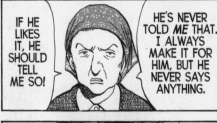

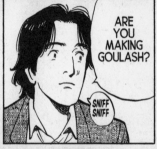

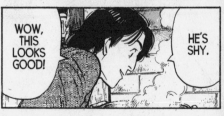

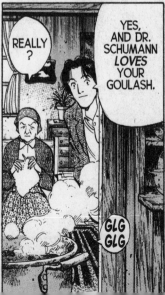

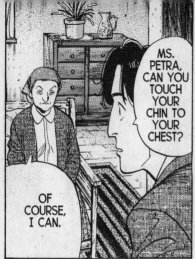

MY SHOULDERS ARE STIFF.
AND I STILL HAVE A LOT OF FOOD TO PREPARE.
STIFF SHOULDERS...?
MS. PETRA, CAN YOU TOUCH YOUR CHIN TO YOUR CHEST?
OF COURSE, I CAN.
SEE... *OWW!*
EXCUSE ME.
?
FOUR FINGERS WIDE...

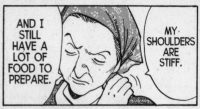

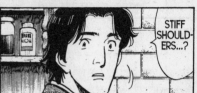

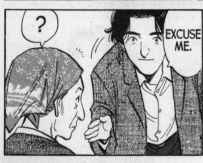

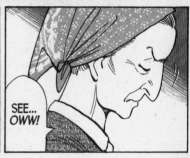

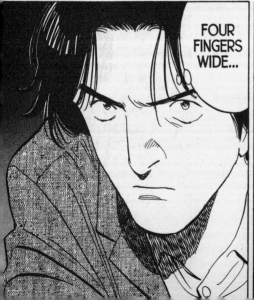

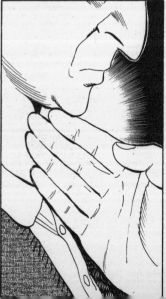

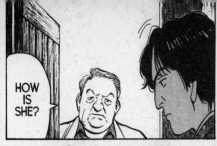

HOW IS SHE?
NOT GOOD...
I'M AFRAID IT'S A SUB-ARACHNOID HEMORRHAGE.
WHAT DOES THAT MEAN?
OH, NOTHING...
ドサ...
WHAT ?!
PETRA !!

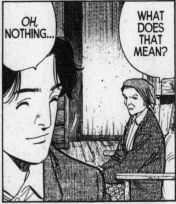

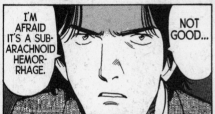

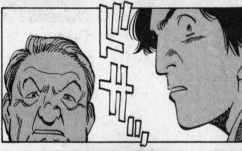

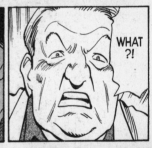

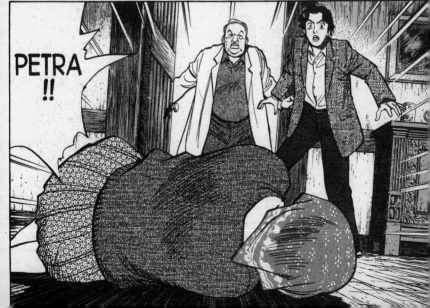

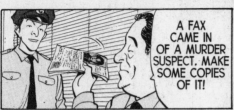

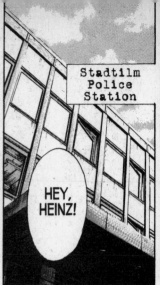

Stadtilm Police Station
HEY, HEINZ!
A FAX CAME IN OF A MURDER SUSPECT. MAKE SOME COPIES OF IT!
HOW'S YOUR MOM? SHE COLLAPSED A FEW DAYS BACK, RIGHT?
SHE'S OKAY. THANKS FOR ASKING.
SHE WOULDN'T DIE, EVEN IF YOU KILLED HER...
!!
THE FIRST STROKE OCCURRED LESS THAN 72 HOURS AGO...

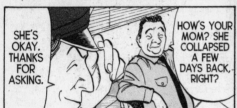

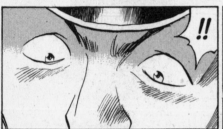

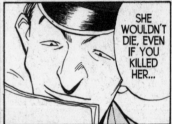

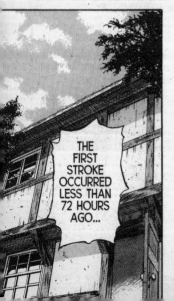

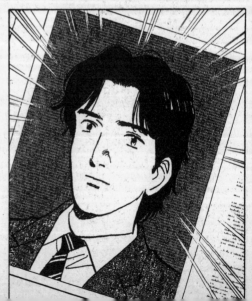

WE CAN STILL MAKE IT! SHE NEEDS SURGERY NOW!!

CAN WE GET A HELI-COPTER?!

WHAT?

CAN *YOU* DO IT...?

IF NOT, I'LL...

PLEASE DO IT, IF YOU CAN.

...

I'LL LOSE ANOTHER PERSON I LOVE BECAUSE OF MY OWN STUPIDITY!!

ARE YOU SURE IT'S HIM?!
YES! HE SAID HIS NAME WAS CHAN, BUT I *KNOW* IT'S HIM!!
HE WAS IN POSER VILLAGE AT *MIELKE'S* RESTAURANT!!
HE STILL MIGHT BE AROUND. SET UP CHECKPOINTS ALONG THE HIGHWAY!!
THIS WILL BE BIG IF WE CATCH HIM, HEINZ!!
Y-YES, SIR!
PREPARE FOR EMER-GENCY DEPLOY-MENT!!
THIS IS GREAT!!
I COULD GET A PROMO-TION!!
I WON'T HAVE TO PATROL THE FIELDS ANYMORE...
FIVE YEARS OF THAT IS ENOUGH!
HEY, HEINZ. TELE-PHONE.

Chapter 7 Petra and Heinz

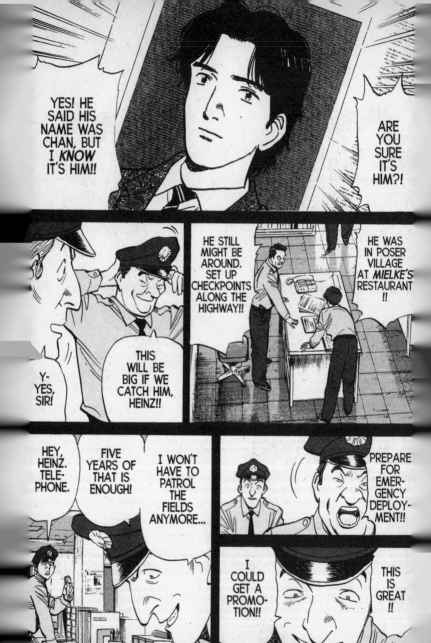

THANKS ...
HURRY IT UP, THOUGH! WE'RE LEAVING!!
WE'LL SEE ABOUT THAT ATTITUDE AFTER MY PROMOTION.
WHAT ?
OH, NOTH-ING.
THIS IS HEINZ.
THE NURSE FROM THE CLINIC?
WHAT ?!
MY MOTHER COLLAPSED AGAIN?!
WE DON'T HAVE A CT SCANNER HERE, ONLY AN X-RAY.
WE DON'T HAVE THE NECESSARY TOOLS FOR BRAIN SURGERY!

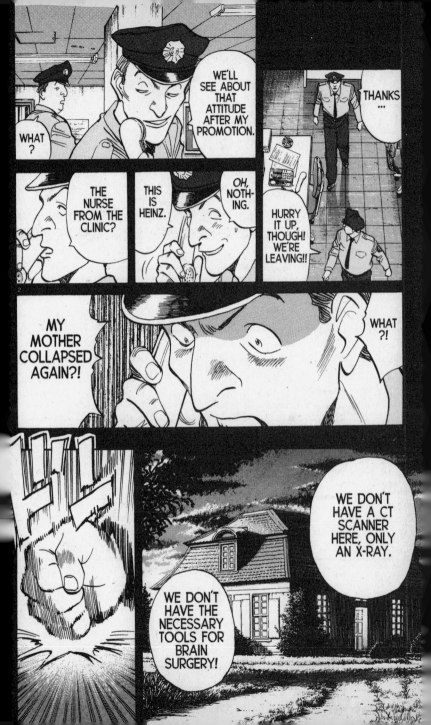

I SHOULD'VE FORCED HER TO GO TO THE HOSPITAL IN KRUPP AFTER THE FIRST STROKE.
BUT NOW...
Chapter 7
Petra and Heinz
YOU'RE MY ONLY HOPE, DR. TENMA
...

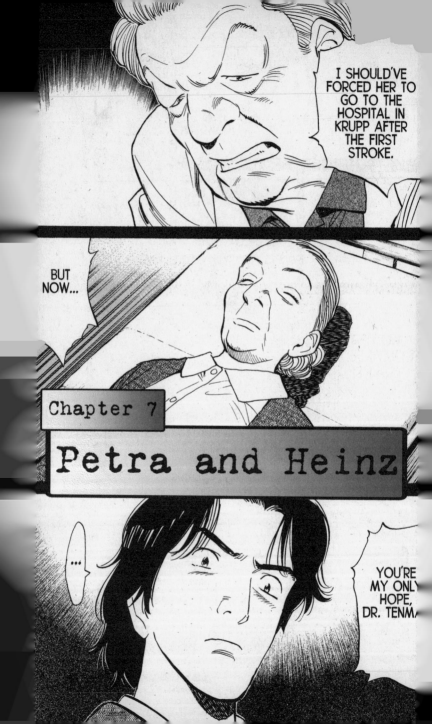

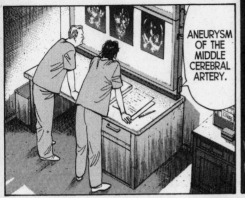

ANEURYSM OF THE MIDDLE CEREBRAL ARTERY.
DAMN IT! WE DON'T EVEN HAVE A SURGICAL MICROSCOPE OR A CRANIO-TOME...
I CAN DO IT. I JUST NEED AN ANEURYSM CLIP.
IT'S TOO DIFFICULT-- EVEN FOR YOU.
カッ
THERE'S NO OTHER CHOICE.
IF THE ANEURYSM RUPTURES, SHE'S NOT GOING TO MAKE IT.
THIS IS ALL MY FAULT.
DR. SCHU-MANN...
THIS ISN'T LIKE YOU. UNTIL NOW, YOU'VE SINGLE-HANDEDLY TAKEN CARE OF THIS TOWN!

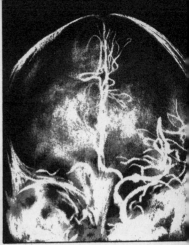

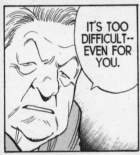

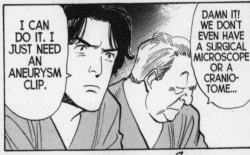

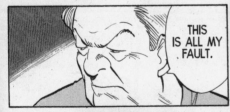

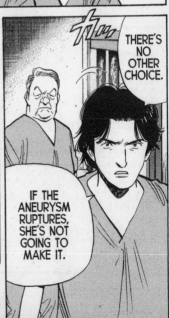

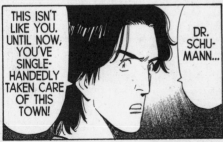

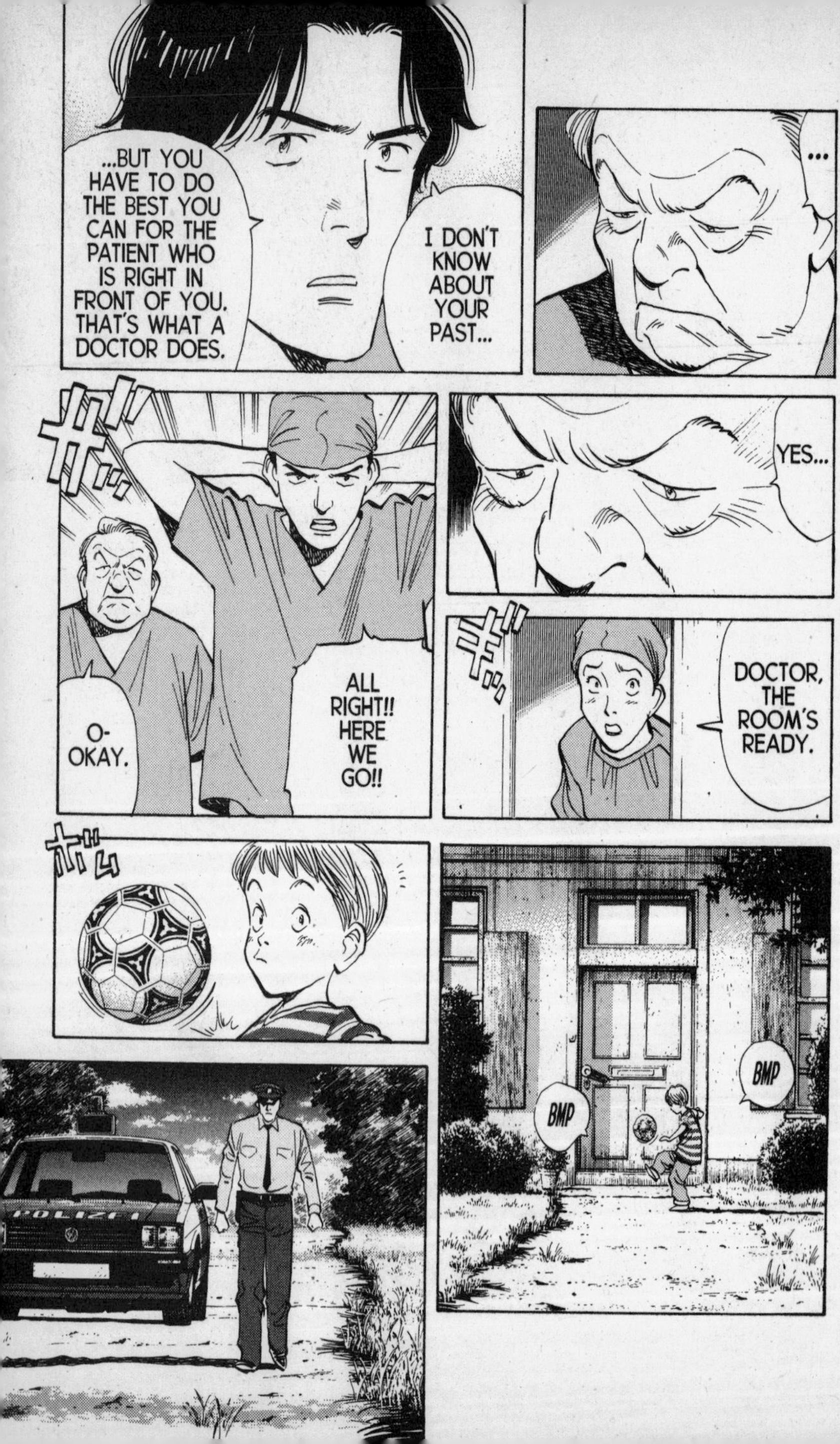
I DON'T KNOW ABOUT YOUR PAST...
...BUT YOU HAVE TO DO THE BEST YOU CAN FOR THE PATIENT WHO IS RIGHT IN FRONT OF YOU. THAT'S WHAT A DOCTOR DOES.
...
YES...
DOCTOR, THE ROOM'S READY.
ALL RIGHT!! HERE WE GO!!
O-OKAY.
BMP
BMP

IS DR. SCHUMANN INSIDE?
YEAH, HE'S OPERATING.
OPERATING? ON MY MOTHER?
THEY'RE OPERATING HERE?!
IT'S OKAY, TENMA'S HERE.
WHAT ...?
TENMA ?!
BEEP
BEEP
BEEP

OPENING THE SKULL.
BP AND PULSE?
BP 126/84, PULSE 88.
DOCTOR, YOU MUST KEEP THE HEAD PERFECTLY STILL.
R-RIGHT.
I'VE NEVER OPERATED WITHOUT THE PROPER EQUIPMENT.
THIS MUST BE HOW THINGS WERE DONE A LONG TIME AGO.
MY GOD, HE DOESN'T EVEN HAVE A CRANIOTOME...
...AND YET HE'S WORKING SO FAST.
!!

HEINZ!! WHAT ARE YOU--?
I CALLED HIM, DR...
!!
WHAT ARE YOU DOING?!
WE'RE OPERATING ON YOUR MOTHER!!
WHAT DO YOU THINK *YOU'RE* DOING?! GET OUT!!
HANDS UP, TENMA!!
...
DO YOU WANT TO KILL YOUR MOTHER?!
HE'S GONNA KILL HER!! TENMA IS WANTED FOR MURDER!!

WHA--?!
...
...
HE KILLED A MAN IN HEIDELBERG...
...AND HE'S THE PRIME SUSPECT FOR THOSE SERIAL MURDERS!
WHO WOULD'VE THOUGHT I'D FIND YOU HERE?
MY COLLEAGUES HAVE A CHECKPOINT SET UP...
I THOUGHT I WAS GOING TO MISS OUT ON ALL THE ACTION...
...BUT MOTHER'S GIVEN ME A SECOND CHANCE!
NOW, HANDS UP!!
...OR I'LL SHOOT!!!
GET OUT OF HERE, HEINZ!!
!!

THIS IS A STERILE ROOM! YOU'RE PUTTING YOUR MOTHER AT RISK!
SHE COULD DIE FROM MENINGITIS!!
THEN ...
THEN STOP THE SURGERY!!
DO YOU REALLY WANT YOUR MOTHER TO DIE?
WHA --?
YOUR MOTHER HAS A SUBARACH-NOID HEMOR-RHAGE.
SHE FIRST COLLAPSED THREE DAYS AGO. SHE MUST BE TREATED WITHIN 72 HOURS.
YOU NEED TO STAY OUT OF THE WAY!

YOU--
YOU'RE USING HER AS A HOSTAGE?!
YOU'RE USING MY MOTHER AS A HOSTAGE!!
WHA --?!
CEREBRAL CLIP AND CLAMP.
...
CEREBRAL CLIP AND CLAMP!!
Y- YES, DR....
TH- THAT'S MY MOTHER !!
DON'T TOUCH HER!!
THAT'S RIGHT. SHE'S YOUR MOTHER.
WHAT HAVE YOU DONE FOR HER THESE PAST FIVE YEARS?
...

HAVE YOU SEEN HER SINCE YOU LEFT TOWN?
SHE'S SACRIFICED A LOT FOR YOU, AND WHAT HAVE YOU DONE IN RETURN?
...
LOOK ...
PEOPLE... DON'T STAY WITH US FOREVER...
...
REMEMBER YOUR MOTHER'S GOULASH?
...
SHE STILL MAKES A PORTION FOR YOU.
I'VE BEEN EATING IT. I *LOVE* THAT GOULASH!

DR. TENMA IS FIGHTING TO SAVE YOUR MOTHER'S LIFE.
IF YOU WANT TO TASTE THAT GOULASH AGAIN...
AGH!!
LET US GET ON WITH IT!!
UGH!!
GRR...
SEE? IT'S OKAY. TENMA'S IN THERE.
DAMN IT...

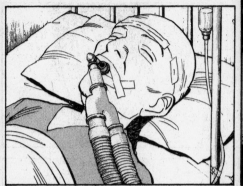

BP 140/86, PULSE 82.
VITAL SIGNS ARE STABLE.
THANK YOU FOR YOUR HELP. GO GET SOME REST.
BUT, DR.--
IT'S OKAY. I'LL BE FINE.
YES, SIR.
DR. TENMA, YOU GET SOME REST, TOO.
NO, I'M OKAY.
WHAT DO YOU MEAN? YOU WERE IN SURGERY FOR THREE HOURS!!

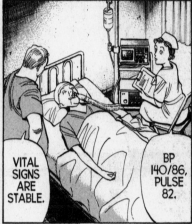

I WANT TO MAKE SURE SHE MAKES IT.
THAT WAY, WHEN MS. PETRA GETS WELL, YOU CAN PROPOSE TO HER.
WHA--?!
WHAT DO YOU MEAN, "PROPOSE"?
I THOUGHT YOU WERE ASLEEP!
I WON'T SLEEP UNTIL I TAKE HIM IN!!
...
AND WHAT'S THIS TALK ABOUT PROPOSING? YOU'RE NOT--
DON'T BE STUPID !!
DON'T BE STUPID ...

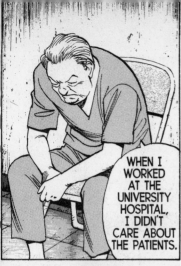

I'M...
I'M NOT WORTHY OF PROPOSING TO ANYONE.
WHEN I WORKED AT THE UNIVERSITY HOSPITAL, I DIDN'T CARE ABOUT THE PATIENTS.
I WAS INTERESTED IN MOVING UP. I GOT IN THE DIRECTOR'S CIRCLE, WROTE HIS PAPERS...
I EVEN MARRIED HIS DAUGHTER.
I MOVED EVEN FURTHER UP THE LADDER.
I DIDN'T PAY ANY ATTENTION TO MY WIFE.
IF I HAD, I WOULD HAVE REALIZED... IF I WERE A REAL DOCTOR...
...?

SLIGHT FEVER, FATIGUE--MY WIFE HAD THE SYMPTOMS OF THE COMMON COLD.
BUT IF I WERE WATCHING CLOSELY, I WOULD HAVE SEEN IT.
SHE HAD CIRRHOSIS. EVENTUALLY, HER LIVER FAILED.
BEFORE HER LAST BREATH, SHE SAID TO ME...
"I FINALLY HAVE YOUR UNDIVIDED ATTENTION..."
I DON'T DESERVE TO LOVE ANYONE.

THAT'S NOT TRUE.
YOU'VE BEEN PAYING ATTENTION ...
YOU'VE BEEN WATCHING OVER THIS WHOLE TOWN.
MS. PETRA IS GOING TO LIVE BECAUSE YOU WERE WATCHING HER.
CHIRP
CHIRP CHIRP

ARE YOU STILL GOING TO TAKE HIM IN?
...
HE DID EVERYTHING TO SAVE YOUR MOTHER.
STILL THINK HE'S A MURDERER?
HEINZ!!
HEINZ!!

CHIEF, THIS IS HEINZ...
HEINZ !!
I'M SORRY, CHIEF. I MADE A MISTAKE ABOUT TENMA.
WE SHOULD CANCEL THE SEARCH.
!!
THE MAN TURNED OUT TO REALLY BE DR. CHAN.
I THOUGHT IT WAS TENMA BECAUSE HE'S ASIAN.
YES, THAT'S RIGHT..
YES, SIR. I'M SORRY.

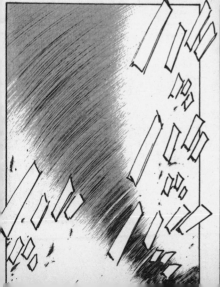

THE STATE DOCTOR WAS SURE SURPRISED.
HE DIDN'T EXPECT SUCH AMAZING TREATMENT FROM A RURAL CLINIC LIKE OURS.
YOU'RE GOING TO LET THAT YOUNG DOCTOR GO?
?
I WAS GOING TO MAKE YOU GUYS A GOOD MEAL, BUT HE PACKED HIS BAGS AND LEFT WITH THE KID.
WHAT?!
WHICH WAY DID HE GO?!
TOWARDS THE HIGHWAY.

DR. TENMA!!
THIS TOWN IS SAFE FOR YOU!!
YOU DON'T HAVE TO RUN!!
HUF
HUF
DR. SCHUMANN!!
DIETER, COME. YOU LIKE IT HERE, DON'T YOU?
YES, THIS MIGHT BE A GOOD PLACE FOR DIETER.
NOT ONLY DIETER. WE CAN HIDE YOU FROM THE POLICE.
...
HELP ME TAKE CARE OF THESE PEOPLE.
THIS TOWN NEEDS YOU.

I MUST GO.
TENMA, I'M GOING WITH YOU!!
WAIT, DIETER!!
WHY ?!
WHY RISK LEAVING ?!
PLEASE TAKE GOOD CARE OF DIETER.
TENMA !!
WAIT, DR. TENMA!!
SHUF
TOGETHER WE CAN SAVE MANY LIVES HERE. WHAT DO YOU SAY?
SAVE LIVES...

I... MUST KILL A MAN.
WHA --?!
WHAT ?
TENMA !!
WHAT ARE YOU SAYING?!
YOU'RE INCAPABLE OF KILLING!!
YOU FIGHT HARD TO *SAVE* LIVES!!
DR. TENMA !!

HE'S GOING.
!!
HE'S REALLY GOING...
...
GO WITH HIM, DIETER.
HUH?
HE WON'T GO ON THE WRONG PATH IF YOU'RE WITH HIM.
LOOK AFTER HIM.
GO!!

YOU AGAIN?!
WHAT IS THIS NONSENSE?
IT DOESN'T MATTER HOW MANY TIMES YOU ASK ME. I'M TELLING YOU THE TRUTH.
COUNCILMAN BOLTZMANN DID NOT HAVE AN AFFAIR WITH A PROSTITUTE!
NOR DID HE MURDER ONE! HE'S NOT INVOLVED!!
PLEASE LEAVE OR I'LL HAVE TO TAKE ACTION.
ACTION...? WOULD YOU SUE FOR DEFAMATION?
NO, YOU WOULDN'T DARE.
IT WOULDN'T BE GOOD FOR A CANDIDATE OF THE GERMAN DEMOCRATIC PARTY TO BE CONNECTED WITH A CRIME LIKE THIS. ESPECIALLY IF THIS STORY HITS THE PAPERS...
IS THAT A THREAT?

Chapter 8 Left Behind

OF COURSE NOT.
I JUST WANT TO KNOW THE TRUTH.

Chapter 8
Left Behind

HE'S TOUGH.
THAT'S WHY HE'S SECRETARY TO A POLITICAL BIG SHOT.
HE'LL COME AROUND.
BUT INSPECTOR LUNGE...
...DO YOU REALLLY THINK A BIG-TIME POLITICIAN WOULD BE INVOLVED WITH A COMMON PROSTITUTE?
SHE WASN'T JUST A COMMON PROSTITUTE...
TAP TAP
SHE USED TO BE A FAVORITE OF KLEIN, THE EXTREMELY WEALTHY FINANCIER. SHE WAS ALSO CONNECTED TO MANY OTHER POLITICIANS AND BUSINESSMEN.
SHE WAS A HIGH-CLASS CALL GIRL WHO MADE OVER 5,000 MARKS A NIGHT.

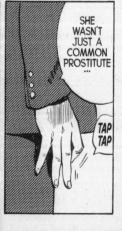

BUT ONLY ONE PERSON CLAIMS TO HAVE SEEN HER IN THE HOTEL WHERE BOLTZMANN STAYS IN BERLIN.
THAT DOESN'T PROVE THEIR RELATION-SHIP.
HAVE YOU DECODED HER CLIENT LIST?
UH, I HAVEN'T DECIPHERED THE CODE YET.
I'LL DO IT. GIVE ME THE DISK.
BUT AREN'T YOU BUSY WITH THE SERIAL MURDERS AT REICHNER PARK?
I DON'T MIND. I'LL DO IT.
INSPECTOR LUNGE, I'VE BEEN WANTING TO ASK YOU...
I HOPE YOU DON'T MIND...
WHAT IS IT?
STRUT
STRUT
WHEN DO YOU SLEEP?
DO YOU EVER GO HOME?

WHAT DOES THAT HAVE TO DO WITH THE CASE?
HUH?
THAT'S AN ILLOGICAL QUESTION.
STRUT
STRUT
...
DID YOU TALK TO HIM?
IT DOESN'T MATTER. HE STOPPED LISTENING TO ME A LONG TIME AGO.
BUT THE SOONER THE BETTER, MOTHER!
SHH! QUIET.
HE'S IN HIS ROOM.
OH...
HOW UN-USUAL.

TAP
TAP TAP
TAP TAP
TAP TAP
TAP TAP
TAP TAP
TAP TAP
BKA Headquarters, Wiesbaden
LUNGE, ARE YOU STILL WORKING THE PROSTITUTE MURDER-- SNOOPING OUT COUNCILMAN BOLTZMANN?
IS THAT A PROBLEM?
YES, THERE'S A PROBLEM! WE'RE GETTING PRESSURE FROM THE GERMAN DEMOCRATIC PARTY *AND* THE MINISTRY OF THE INTERIOR.

DON'T DIG TOO DEEP. I'M TELLING YOU FOR YOUR OWN GOOD.
JUST SMOOTH IT OUT LIKE YOU ALWAYS DO, CHIEF.
I CAN'T WITH THIS ONE.
DO WHAT YOU CAN.
STRUT
LUNGE!
WHAT IF YOU'RE WRONG?!
YOU'LL LOSE EVERYTHING !!
YOU'VE GOT A GREAT CAREER. YOU DON'T WANT TO LOSE IT ALL FOR A LITTLE FAME.
OR ARE YOU DOING THIS IN THE NAME OF JUSTICE?
FAME...
JUSTICE ...
I'M NOT INTERESTED IN EITHER.
?

A WOMAN WAS MURDERED.
I'M OUT TO FIND THE KILLER. THAT'S ALL.
STRUT
STRUT
LUNGE !!
TAP
TAP
INSPECTOR LUNGE, YOU HAVE A GUEST...
TAP
GOT IT.
WHAT?
I'VE FIGURED OUT THE CODE. USE THIS FORMULA TO GET ALL THE NAMES ON THE CLIENT LIST.

UH, RIGHT...
THERE'S A WOMAN HERE TO SEE YOU...
IT'S EVA HEINEMANN...
ガッ
HEY!! Y-YOU CAN'T COME IN HERE...
WHAT ARE YOU DOING, INSPECTOR LUNGE?!
I GAVE YOU THE INFORMATION YOU NEEDED!!
WHEN ARE YOU GOING TO ARREST TENMA?!

YOU'VE BEEN DRINKING...
HOW CAN I NOT WHEN YOU STUPID COPS CAN'T SOLVE A SIMPLE CASE?!
I'VE SOLVED DR. TENMA'S CASE.
...
THE DIRECTOR'S MURDER TEN YEARS AGO, THE SERIAL MURDER OF MIDDLE-AGED COUPLES--TENMA SAID THAT JOHAN IS RESPONSIBLE FOR IT ALL.
THIS JOHAN IS JUST ANOTHER PERSON-ALITY WITHIN TENMA.
WITH THIS SUPPOSITION, WHAT SEEMED ILLOGICAL NOW MAKES SENSE.
ALL WE DO NOW IS WAIT FOR THE POLICE TO CAPTURE HIM.
SO YOUR JOB IS DONE AFTER YOU'VE GOT A WARRANT?
DR. TENMA-- A VERY INTERESTING PERSON.
I'D LOVE TO SIT AND TALK TO HIM.
BUT...
SHUF

I HAVE SO MANY OTHER CASES PILING UP ON MY DESK.
NOW, IF YOU'LL EXCUSE ME.
STRUT
STRUT
DON'T YOU EVER LET UP?!
LEAVE ME ALONE!! I TOLD YOU MR. BOLTZMANN HAS AN ALIBI--
AN ALIBI? OF COURSE HE DOES. THE MURDERER WAS A PROFES-SIONAL.
ARE YOU SAYING MR. BOLTZMANN HIRED A HIT MAN?!
NON-SENSE!
I'VE DECODED THE VICTIM'S LIST OF CLIENTS.
!!

MR. BOLTZMANN'S NAME AND NUMBER IS ON THAT LIST.
...
EVEN IF THAT WERE TRUE...
IT DOESN'T PROVE HE KILLED HER!
TRUE...
I DON'T HAVE TIME FOR THIS!! PLEASE LEAVE!!
THERE'S NOT ENOUGH EVIDENCE, INSPECTOR.
ARE YOU FAMILIAR WITH A PUBLISHER CALLED SHELL-HOURNE?
!!
?
THEY'RE NOT A MAJOR COMPANY-- NOT VERY WELL KNOWN...
THEY PUBLISH TELL-ALL BOOKS ABOUT CELEBRITIES. THAT'S HOW THEY STAY IN BUSINESS.
THAT COMPANY PLAYS VERY DIRTY.

THEY HIRE WOMEN TO GET CLOSE TO FAMOUS PEOPLE IN ORDER TO CREATE SCANDALS TO WRITE ABOUT.
IF I WERE YOU, I'D WATCH OUT FOR PEOPLE LIKE THAT.
SHUF
...
SHUF
UH...IN-SPECTOR LUNGE !!
KOFF ...
RETCH !!

SHUF
SHUF
SHUF
CREAK
TAP
TAP
SLAM

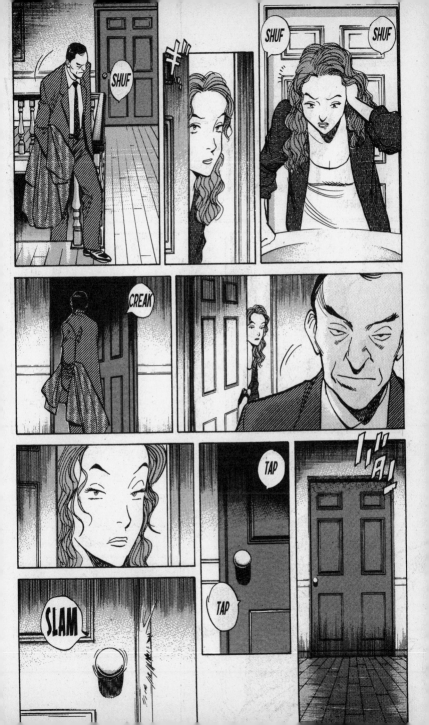

IT WAS LIKE A CHECKMATE!
THE SECRETARY COULDN'T EVEN RESPOND!
HOW DID INSPECTOR LUNGE FIND OUT ABOUT THAT PUBLISHER?
HE'S UNBELIEVABLE.
HE DOESN'T EVER REST. HE'S SUPERHUMAN.
SUPERHUMAN IS RIGHT.
HE DOESN'T SEEM TO HAVE ANY HUMAN SIDE TO HIM.
HUH?!
OH! THAT'S CHECKMATE!!
HEY, DON'T BUTT INTO OUR GAME...
OH--
DON'T WASTE TIME WITH BORING GAMES.

A LITTLE THREAT AND THE PRESIDENT OF THAT PUBLISHING COMPANY CONFESSED. WRITE THIS UP!
Y-YES, SIR!
WHAT DO YOU THINK THIS MEMO IS?
IT'S THE CALL GIRL'S NOTEBOOK. IT RECORDS THE DATE, TIME, AND OTHER DETAILS OF HER ENCOUNTERS WITH A CERTAIN CLIENT.
THE MAN IN QUESTION IS ONLY REFERRED TO BY THE LETTER "B."
HER NOTES ARE QUITE INTERESTING. IT READS LIKE A NOVEL.
NOT TO MENTION, SHELLHOURNE PUBLISHING HAD A CONTRACT WITH HER FOR HER AUTO-BIOGRAPHY.

OH, YES... HAVE YOU EVER BEEN IN CONTACT WITH A MAN NAMED YANKER?
HE'S A PRO-FESSIONAL KILLER...
GET OUT.
GET THE HELL OUT OF HERE!!

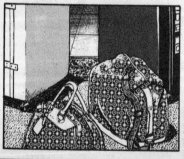

WE'RE LEAVING.
WE'LL COME BACK FOR THE REST OF OUR THINGS LATER.
...
FATHER, DID YOU EVEN NOTICE I WAS PREGNANT?
YOU'RE GOING TO THE MAN WHO FATHERED YOUR CHILD?
I'M LEAVING, TOO.
I BET YOU HAD NO IDEA THAT I WAS HAVING AN AFFAIR.
RRING

LUNGE.
THIS IS BOLTZMANN'S SECRETARY, MINTAG.
I'LL TELL YOU EVERYTHING. JUST GET HERE RIGHT AWAY!
UNDERSTOOD. THANK YOU.
I HAVE TO GO. WE'LL TALK ABOUT THIS LATER.
STRUT
STRUT
?

WHAT'S GOING ON?

IN-SPECTOR!!

HUF HUF

TH-THE SECRETARY...

HE KILLED HIMSELF!

TRUT

STRUT

CHIRP CHIRP

"MR. BOLTZMANN IS INNOCENT."
THAT'S WHAT WAS WRITTEN ON THE NOTE THE SECRETARY LEFT BEHIND.
LUNGE, I'M HANDING THIS ONE OVER TO INSPECTOR KAMINSKI...
...AS WELL AS THE REICHNER PARK AND GALLAND CASES.
WHAT'S LEFT FOR ME?

I HAVE NOTHING FOR YOU...

STRUT

STRUT

STRUT

STRUT

STRUT

STRUT

SHF

YOU'RE ALL I HAVE LEFT.

UM... IN-SPECTOR?
CREAK
YOU HAVE A GUEST.
EVA HEINEMANN AGAIN...
SHOW HER IN!

about the author

Naoki Urasawa, born in Tokyo in 1960, is Japan's manga master of the suspense thriller. Critically acclaimed and immensely popular, his award-winning works include *20th Century Boys*, *Master Keaton*, *Pineapple Army*, and *Yawara*.

159.7—FX: Bomu (bump)

161.6—FX: Ba (fwoosh)

167.2—FX: Ga (grab)

167.4—FX: Batamu (slam)

173.7—FX: Gi (creak)

174.7—FX: Ba ba ba ba
(helicopter propeller)

175.1—FX: Ba ba ba ba
(helicopter propeller)

175.2—FX: Ba ba ba ba
(helicopter propeller)

178.4—FX: Za (shuf)

178.7—FX: Za (shuf)

178.8—FX: Da (dash)

Chapter 8

188.5—FX: Gi (creak)

189.3—FX: Ka (footstep)

194.2—FX: Gi (creak)

194.6—FX: Batan (slam)

195.1—FX: Kan (slam)

195.5—FX: Kan (slam)

199.4—FX: Ba (fwap)

199.6—FX: Batan (slam)

199.8—FX: Paho Paho (siren)

200.1—FX: Paho (siren)

200.4—FX: Paho Paho (siren)

glossary

Chapter 1

7.4—Ta (footstep)

7.7—Ta (feet landing)

12.2—FX: Ta (feet landing)

12.6—FX: Da (dash)

20.3—FX: Batan (door shutting)

20.6—FX: Dota dota (thud thud)

27.2—FX: Pan (gunshot)

27.4—FX: Gi (creak)

29.2—FX: Gata (clatter)

Chapter 2

32.4—FX: Ba (fwip)

33.7—FX: Don (shove)

34.3—FX: Buon (vroom)

34.7—FX: Gi (creak)

48.4—FX: Ba (fwip)

Chapter 3

64.7—FX: Ba (fwip)

71.3—FX: Gi (creak)

75.6—FX: Gara gara (rattle rattle)

76.1—FX: Bon bon (kick kick)

76.7—FX: Don don (knock knock)

77.1—FX: Ba (fwoosh)

77.3—FX: Da (dash)

Chapter 4

82.1—FX: Ba (fwoosh)

83.7—FX: Ba (swoop)

84.3—FX: Gi (creak)

84.8—FX: Da da da (tmp tmp tmp; dashing down stairs)

85.3—FX: Ka ka ka (footsteps)

90.1—FX: Ka (footstep)

Chapter 5

108.2—FX: Da (dash)

109.1—FX: Ba (fwoosh)

117.5—FX: Bo (burst into flames)

121.1—FX: Ba (fwoosh)

126.2—FX: Ba (fwoosh)

126.3—FX: Ba (fwoosh)

127.5—FX: Gasha (clatter)

127.6—FX: Go (bam)

129.2—FX: Za (hoist)

129.9—FX: Pon (kick)

Chapter 6

131.2—FX: Don don (knock knock)

132.1—FX: Don don (knock knock)

132.2—FX: Don don (knock knock)

133.5—FX: Ba ba ba (put put put)

133.6—FX: Ba ba ba (put put put)

134.1—FX: Ba ba ba ba ba ba (put put put)

134.3—FX: Ba ba ba ba (put put put)

136.6—FX: Gi (creak)

137.1—FX: Bamu (slam)

137.5—FX: Hagu hagu (chomp chomp)

138.4—FX: Hagu hagu (chomp chomp)

139.3—FX: Basa (fwap)

142.6—FX: Gi (creak)

142.7—FX: Batan (slam)

146.5—FX: Za (shuf)

152.5—FX: Dosa (fwump)

Chapter 7

156.7—FX: Don (bam)

158.5—FX: Ka (footstep)

159.4—FX: Gi (creak)

159.5—FX: Za (shuf)

NAOKI URASAWA'S
MONSTER
Could you
become a killer..
VIZ MEDIA
www.viz.com
© 1995 Naoki URASAWA Studio Nuts/Shogakukan Inc.

NAOKI URASAWA'S
MONSTER
...to catch a killer?
NAOKI URASAWA'S MONSTER
FROM JAPAN'S MASTER OF SUSPENSE
"Dark and engrossing, this is more than a hardboiled story—it's an entire world of its own."
–Steve Hamilton, Edgar Award-winning author of Ice Run
volume 4
FIND OUT AT MONSTER.VIZ.COM
MAKE A CHOICE. PAY THE PRICE.
viz media
www.viz.com
© 1995 Naoki URASAWA Studio Nuts/Shogakukan Inc.